Born in 1959 in Hemel Hempstead, Dougie Brimson left school and enlisted in the RAF where he trained as a mechanical engineer. After serving for over eighteen years and attaining the rank of sergeant, he left the forces in 1994 to pursue a career as a writer.

Following the co-authorship of four non-fiction books examining the culture of football hooliganism, Dougie struck out on his own and made the move into fiction with the Lynda La Plante-inspired thriller *The Crew*.

The following year, he delivered another non-fiction examination of football and its culture, *Barmy Army*, and followed this book first with *Billy's Log* – a comic novel about single males – and then a second thriller, *Top Dog*. A year later, the murders of two Leeds United fans in Istanbul provided the motivation for *Eurotrashed*, a hard-hitting examination of hooliganism across Europe.

Screenwriting credits include the critically acclaimed short *It's a Casual Life* and the full-length feature *Green Street*.

He has been happily married to Tina since 1983 and they have three grown-up children.

Also by Dougie Brimson

The Geezers Guide to Football
The Crew
Billy's Log
Top Dog
Eurotrashed
Barmy Army
Everywhere We Go (with Eddy Brimson)
England, My England (with Eddy Brimson)
Capital Punishment (with Eddy Brimson)
Derby Days (with Eddy Brimson)

KICKING OFF

Why Hooliganism and Racism are Killing Football

Dougie Brimson

headline

First published in 2006
by HEADLINE BOOK PUBLISHING

1

Cataloguing in Publication Data is available from the British Library

0 7553 1432 8 (ISBN-10)
978 0 7553 1432 4 (ISBN-13)

Typeset in Stone Sans by Avon DataSet Ltd,
Bidford-on-Avon, Warwickshire

Text design by Ben Cracknell Studios

Printed and bound in Great Britain by
Mackays of Chatham plc, Chatham, Kent

Headline's policy is to use papers that are natural, renewable and
recyclable products and made from wood grown in sustainable
forests. The logging and manufacturing processes are expected to
conform to the environmental regulations of the country of origin.

HEADLINE BOOK PUBLISHING
A division of Hodder Headline
338 Euston Road
London NW1 3BH

www.headline.co.uk
www.hodderheadline.com

For Tina, Rebecca, Kayleigh, Ben, Lee
and our beautiful granddaughter Betty.

CONTENTS

ACKNOWLEDGEMENTS

With huge thanks to David and Juliana at Headline for their patience and everyone who helped out, especially Pete F, Alabama Paul and numerous others who shall remain nameless by choice. Also big thanks to Banksy at solarradio.com for the sounds that kept me going!

But most of all, thanks to Tina and Karen for the frequent motivational talks!

KICKING OFF

INTRODUCTION

In 1968, when I was a mere nine years old, an event took place which ended up shaping my life – my dad took me to football.

As it happens, it ended up being the only game he ever took me to and, somewhat bizarrely given that in his youth he was a bit of a footie fan himself, he didn't even take me to watch his beloved Spurs. Instead, he took me to watch our local side, Watford, then a lowly second division outfit.

The game in question was against Bristol Rovers and finished up as a 1–0 win for the Hornets, but for me, sitting in a freezing cold and half-empty Shrodell's stand, it was tedious in the extreme. Even though, like most kids back then, if I wasn't at school or asleep I was kicking a ball around, I really couldn't see the attraction of paying to watch someone else playing the game and, given that the old man showed even less inclination to take me back than I ever had of going, the professional game and I stayed strangers for a few years.

The 1970 Cup final changed that forever. My brother Ed had somehow developed a strange affinity for Leeds United, and me, being a typical pain-in-the-arse older brother, chose to cheer for Chelsea simply to piss him off. It worked. More importantly, as a result of this game, me and my mate Clive began to sneak off to Stamford Bridge, where I not only discovered the delights of watching live football, I fell in love with it.

However, for a variety of reasons mostly connected with a

reluctance to get the shit kicked out of me by any of the marauding nutters who haunted London's Underground network each and every Saturday back in the early seventies, I soon ended up back at Vicarage Road and, by 1975, at the tender age of sixteen, was a confirmed disciple of the Golden Boys. I've been one ever since.

In all honesty, I am incredibly grateful for this. After all, one of the reasons I started going to games in the first place was to escape into a world devoid of family and, although these days parents and brothers have been replaced by wife and daughters, the basic reason for going remains the same. The fact that I can share those experiences with my son is an added bonus, even though he now shuns the company of his old man for that of his own mates once we leave our favoured public house!

And what experiences they have been. From the incredible highs of the Elton John and Graham Taylor era to the nightmare periods under Dave Bassett and Gianluca Vialli, the ride on the emotional rollercoaster that is football fandom, which began when I first walked into Vicarage Road over thirty years ago, has certainly been more interesting than most. It has also given me plenty to talk, think and write about.

However, much as I love the Golden Boys, like most people who support a club that enjoys only fleeting periods of success, many of my feelings towards them are negative ones, born mostly, out of frustration, anger and disappointment. In truth, I have always found this to be one of the more liberating aspects of fandom, because, as a natural pessimist, not only do I like a good moan, I also bear a grudge. And thirty-odd years following Watford has certainly given me an ample supply of grudges. Most of these would be regarded as both pointless and irrational by anyone who isn't a football fan, but will be instantly recognisable to anyone who is.

For example, until the day I die I will continue to wish nothing but ill fortune on our former manager Glenn Roeder, because in 1996, despite repeated assurances that he would never bring a former L*t*n T*wn player to the club, he ended up signing one. Not just any old one either, but their former striker and self-confessed Scum fan Kerry Dixon. As a result, like many Hornets at the time, I refused to attend games while he was in the squad, because the very idea of him wearing a yellow shirt, my yellow shirt, made me feel nauseous.

Similarly, to this day the mere sight of a certain steward at Vicarage Road brings forth an expletive or two, because about five years ago he refused to let me leave a freezing cold home end and go to the warmth and comfort of the main sponsor's box, despite the fact that my invite came direct from the head of the company who could clearly be seen gesturing me up. Bastard.

I have dozens like that and others not limited to Watford. My supporting years have equipped me with a dislike of people ranging from ex-Liverpool striker John Aldridge through to *Soccer AM* presenter Helen Chamberlain, together with a hatred of numerous clubs, including Oldham, Crystal Palace and Grays Athletic. Like I say, I bear a grudge.

Grudges are, however, limiting in one specific respect. They are very personal. While I know why I don't like the so-called comedians Reeves and Mortimer, no one else does and even if they did, I doubt they would care. Similarly, you can't really have a grudge about the ineptitude of the authorities or the exploitation of hooliganism by academics, but you can have both a moan and an opinion. And as anyone who knows me will testify, I love a good moan. Indeed, the great joy of writing about football has been that it has allowed me to broaden my moaning horizons and become even more opinionated.

I should stress, though, that many of my opinions are not that different from those you will hear in any pre- or post-match pub on any given Saturday, because, in truth, there isn't much about the game which gets me particularly hot under the collar. For example, I absolutely agree that the wages paid to certain individuals are obscene and believe that the only way the game will ever regain control of this is for the FA to impose a rule whereby clubs can only pay out fifty per cent of their turnover in wages. However, until that time arrives, I have no problem with players taking whatever the clubs are stupid enough to pay them. I certainly would if I were in their shoes.

Similarly, if clubs can get away with charging a fortune to walk through a turnstile then good luck to them. We might believe that we are addicted to our chosen team and therefore have no choice but to take our places each and every matchday, but of course we're not. It's down to personal choice. I also believe that, aside from a few obvious exceptions, the Premiership is hugely overrated and while it might be lacking in quality, game for game the Championship generally provides far more excitement.

But none of that really concerns me too much. I'm actually more pissed off that they don't sell Pukka pies at Watford, although even this is tempered by the knowledge that if I'm really desperate I can always buy one from the chip shop in Market Street before or after the game.

There are, however, things about our beloved game that I do care passionately about, although they tend to be issues that are universally regarded as being either unsavoury, controversial or dangerous. As a result, they are all too often swept under the carpet in the hope that they will wither and die on their own or, worse, are left to the devices of so-called 'experts', the bulk of whom have nothing but self-interest at heart.

Yet these are issues that, in one way or another, impact on every single football fan and to abdicate responsibility for them is an extremely dangerous thing for the game to do, because by allowing outside agencies to set the agenda you allow them to stifle debate, which in turn allows the problem to fester unchecked.

Sadly, that is the risk the game seems prepared to take, largely, I suspect, because a free and open debate on an issue such as racism would require input from organisations or individuals that would be both controversial and politically sensitive. Inevitably, such a debate would also extend way beyond sport and the game doesn't seem to want any part of that. But of course, if and when things go wrong it is the rank and file football fan who will have to deal with the consequences.

I don't agree with that approach. Not one little bit. As fans, we have carried this game of ours for decades and have dragged it back from the abyss too many times to mention, so it's about time someone in authority shouldered some responsibility and looked after our interests. However, that will only happen when the FA finally realises that there are large numbers of supporters who are increasingly unhappy with some of the outrageous things that are going on in the name of football. Maybe then it will do something about it.

That, in essence, is what this book is about, because I want to raise a fresh awareness of the things I and others believe are fundamentally wrong with our game and provide an alternative side to what, up to now, have been largely one-sided debates. Hopefully, by doing that I can get people thinking and, more importantly, talking.

To be honest, however, this is a book I never thought I would write or, to be more precise, I hoped I would never have to. You see, I've actually been here before. Back in February 2000, I released what I genuinely thought was going to be my last ever non-fiction book. Entitled *Barmy Army*, it charted the evolution of football violence domestically and examined the emergence of a new breed of lad from within the Casual scene. It also gave my opinions on everything from the media to the police and, finally, based on my experiences as a lifelong football fan, a peripheral figure on the Casual scene and someone who had spent years researching among those on all sides, I examined the different ways in which I believed a solution to the hooligan problem could be achieved. Thankfully, it attracted some excellent reviews and was also well received by those people with an interest in the subject, so in many ways I was happy to go out on a reasonable high.

Tragically, just a month after *Barmy Army*'s release and even as I was in the middle of the promotion for it, two Leeds United fans, Chris Loftus and Kevin Speight, were hacked to death outside a bar in the middle of Istanbul. With Euro 2000 fast approaching and concern about hooliganism already high, the press went crazy. It got even worse when Arsenal and Galatasaray supporters were involved in serious disorder in Copenhagen ahead of the UEFA Cup final. There were even calls for England to withdraw from the tournament, for fear of what was going to happen.

Yet what concerned me more than anything was the attitude of certain sections of the media towards the two murders. In some instances, it was all but implied that the lads had basically got what they deserved, simply because they had been in Istanbul the night before their game. Not only did this show absolutely no respect for the grieving families, but, more worryingly, it took the spotlight away from the Turkish authorities who seemed increasingly unwilling to secure any kind of justice for the victims.

Thankfully, as a result of the publicity for *Barmy Army* and the widespread fears about violence in Belgium and Holland, it was a busy time for me media-wise and so at every opportunity I tried to keep the murders in the public eye – not only by reminding people what had happened, but by highlighting the fact that the killers were still at large.

Although this was a very personal thing, it was especially gratifying to receive a lot of support for my stance, particularly from supporters at Elland Road. It also attracted a request to write about what had happened on that fateful night. The fact that it came from someone who had been involved in the actual incident was extremely significant, because it showed that people close to Chris and Kevin were prepared to put their faith in me, sure in the knowledge that I would tell the truth. As a result, I agreed immediately, although only under the proviso that they would be happy for me to include a Turkish perspective on what happened.

That book came out in 2002 and was entitled *Eurotrashed*. Alongside events in Istanbul, it also examined the history of English hooliganism on its travels overseas, as well as the growth and nature of football-related violence across Europe.

Once again, I was extremely lucky in that *Eurotrashed* was also well received, not just in the UK, but across Europe, so I was happy to finally take my writing in another direction, first with the script for a short movie called *It's a Casual Life* and then a full-length screenplay for a film provisionally called *Hooligans*, but which ended up as *Green Street*.

But even as I was enjoying this respite, I kept a wary eye on what was going on, particularly in relation to the two issues that had long interested me the most – hooliganism and racism. And although I really didn't like what I was seeing, what concerned me even more was that no one in authority seemed to be able to see what I could see. Even to most of the lads I know, as well as a few of the more switched-on journalists, it was all blindingly obvious, so why on earth did none of those who administer our game realise what was happening?

Although I had my theories as to why that was, I had absolutely no inclination to get back on the laptop and return to print to give voice to them. I'd said pretty much all I wanted to say on just about everything relating to the world of football fandom and even I was becoming bored with repeating the same warnings and watching them being ignored. At least until they came to pass, which most eventually have, when I would simply say, 'I told you so.'

Then, out of the blue, in 2004 I received an invitation to visit Russia, first to do some promotional work for my publisher Amphora at the Moscow Book Fair and then to take part in a festival of contemporary literature organised by the British Consulate in St Petersburg. Obviously I accepted without hesitation and I'm glad I did, although I have to admit that as an ex-serviceman who spent many years training to defend the West against the might of the Soviet forces, I did travel with a degree of trepidation, as well as a few preconceived ideas about what I would find.

In the event, I have to say that Russia was not what I expected at all and I had an amazing time, although there were certainly plenty of surreal moments. Walking through the gates into the Kremlin and lighting a candle of remembrance at the Piskarevskoe Memorial Cemetery are among a number of things I will remember for the rest of my life. I doubt I will forget eating sliced reindeer tongue and elk liver pâté either, yet what really made the trip for me were the Russian people, whom I found universally friendly and generous, as well as totally open and honest. They were, in many ways, a revelation and I am humbled to say that some of those I met and spent time with have become close and valued friends.

This includes a good few football lads and, if I have one regret about the trip, it's that I didn't get the opportunity to watch a game in their company. I did, however, learn a lot during my time with them, all of which was extremely interesting, but there was one thing that caused me concern and that was the fact that some of them were extremely and unashamedly racist. It was like a throwback to the early eighties.

Although initially I was both shocked and disappointed by their behaviour, I quickly realised that I had no right to cast any judgement upon them and nor does anyone else. Russia is a very different place to the UK, particularly culturally, and it's fair to say that the number of black and Asian faces I saw during my ten-day visit could be counted on the fingers of one hand. Even then, I'd have two left over. In that sense, it's not very different to fifties Britain and we all know what things were like back then.

Thankfully, I met plenty of people who showed me that things are certainly changing in Russia and, while it will take time, I have no doubt they will get there in the end. However, this encounter with a level of racism I hoped I would never see again did have one major consequence – it made me angry. By reminding me how bad things used to be here in England, it served to highlight just how far we have come in this particular battle. Just as importantly, it made me realise that those who have been exploiting the game to further their own ends have been getting away with it unchallenged for far too long. That has to change.

So, as someone who has a profile of sorts, I decided that if anyone was going to speak out, it might as well be me and by the time I landed back at Heathrow I had the basic outline for this book already written. Thankfully, my publishers were keen and so work began in earnest almost immediately. The rest, as they say, is history.

However, while I have little doubt that many of the opinions contained in this book will be regarded as controversial, people must not make the mistake of thinking that I am the only one who holds them. I am not. They are shared by many football fans who, like me, have just had enough. So my hope is that by finally committing them to print it will at the very least kick-start some kind of debate on issues which not only deserve to be debated, but which demand it. Better still, it might even force a change in attitudes.

Since *Kicking Off* is in many ways a continuation of *Barmy Army*, I have also included an update on a few other things relating to football and in particular the terrace culture, not simply because it's a fairly obvious and useful thing to do, but because there are plenty of people who haven't read the previous book and, hopefully, this will entice them to do just that!

Up the 'Orns.

PART ONE
TWENTY-FIRST CENTURY MAYHEM

CHAPTER ONE

EURO 2000 TO 2002

Before we begin to delve too deeply into the issues surrounding the continuing existence of hooliganism, it is vital that we determine the size and severity of the problem as it currently affects the game. After all, if the authorities and the media are to be believed, it isn't really a problem anymore. There are even those who would argue that it hasn't been for some considerable time.

The reality, as we shall soon establish for the benefit of anyone who doesn't actually bother to attend games on a regular basis, is somewhat different. For while we might not suffer the kind of match-day mayhem the nation was forced to endure in the seventies and eighties, the hooligan threat has continued to impact on the game in the twenty-first century, albeit in a different way from those heady days.

So how has that happened? Well, like most questions, the answer can be found in history. Since this was covered at length in *Barmy Army* it would be pointless to go over that ground again, but it is important that we bring things up to date and so at this point I will merely pick up where that book left off; the turn of the century and the fast-approaching Euro 2000.

While not by any means a definitive listing of events, what follows should provide some indication as to the nature, frequency and, in some cases, tragedy, of what goes on week in and week out – all in the name of football.

*

The game headed towards the new millennium in confident and optimistic mood. The Premiership was firmly established as probably the most exciting league in world football and players from across the globe were flocking to England, attracted by the staggering wages on offer and the opportunity to compete against the very best. Even my beloved Watford had clawed its way into the top flight – if only for a single season – thanks to one of the most amazing play-off series I have ever known. Yet behind the euphoria lurked the same old problem; the violent minority.

Things had actually not been going well for a while. The latter part of 1999 had seen increasing concern at the potential for trouble at Euro 2000 and the situation was made worse in the November when the BBC broadcast the now infamous *MacIntyre Undercover* documentary. Although roundly condemned by just about everyone who knew anything about hooliganism, the documentary, in which MacIntyre supposedly infiltrated the so-called Chelsea Head-hunters, succeeded in putting the issue firmly back in the public eye. To make matters worse, just three days after the broadcast a mob of around 700 English lads descended on Glasgow for the Scotland versus England Euro 2000 qualifier. In the event, a massive police operation involving 2000 officers prevented the large-scale disorder many people had forecast, but there were still 170 arrests.

The following week, the Scots descended on London for the return fixture. Again, a huge police operation prevented major incidents, although fifty-six people were injured and thirty-nine arrested during clashes in London's West End, most notably when a group of approximately fifty English lads attacked 300 Scots in Trafalgar Square. It was the last thing the authorities needed, yet over the coming months worse was to come – much, much worse.

In the December, two of the most notorious groups of supporters in football were involved in serious disorder in South East London, when Cardiff City's Soul Crew travelled en masse for the club's visit to Millwall. Always a high-profile fixture, tensions had been heightened by major disturbances in the centre of Cardiff when the two clubs had met on the opening day of the season, yet, if anything, this was worse, as the police were forced to make repeated baton charges on supporters who continually confronted them throughout the day. Among many incidents, a police van was bombarded with missiles as it travelled along Rotherhithe New Road and riot officers had to rescue a second vehicle, which had become surrounded by a hostile mob. Another group of officers was forced to help passengers trapped on a bus, which was being pelted with stones, while at one stage a line of riot police fought with a mob of 200 supporters who had been bombarding them with bricks and wooden poles outside South Bermondsey railway station. In the event, only a large number of reinforcements, including mounted officers, managed to calm the situation, which went on late into the evening.

January saw further serious disorder at Manchester City versus Leeds, Leicester versus West Ham, Wolves versus QPR, Sunderland versus Leeds and Manchester United versus Middlesbrough. There was also violence at the Cambridge United versus Bolton Cup tie, where a man was stabbed in the neck. The last weekend of the month saw numerous and extremely violent clashes in Birmingham city centre, involving fans from Wolves, Birmingham City, Aston Villa, Leeds and Hartlepool.

However, the worst incident that month involved a group of over a hundred Bristol Rovers lads who travelled to their game at Oxford United and became involved in confrontations with police. Afterwards, they were taken to Didcot Station and sent back home, but on arrival over fifty of them headed for a well-known Bristol City pub. Once there, they staged a concerted attack on the building and those inside, smashing all the windows and causing injuries to numerous people. Police from all over the city were drafted in to deal with the subsequent running battles, which resulted in four people being charged with violent disorder.

If anything, things got even worse in February. Within the first few days, Leicester City and Aston Villa fans were involved in serious disturbances, both before and after their game at Filbert Street, but it was on 5 February that things turned really nasty.

On this one day, a huge security operation was required to prevent trouble at the Tottenham versus Chelsea game, where police arrested over eighty Blues fans for breach of the peace and recovered a variety of weapons, including a meat cleaver, a nasal spray bottle filled with ammonia and a variety of knives. Further north, almost 350 Wednesday and United fans clashed in Sheffield in what police were convinced was a prearranged confrontation. One officer suffered a broken jaw as running battles took place throughout the city centre and continued until tactical support was drafted in from outside the city to help calm things down. To make things even worse, at Anfield Leeds fans began fighting with each other and then turned on the stewards and the police in what senior officers remain convinced was a premeditated attack. In the end, reinforcements had to enter the ground and draw batons to prevent things getting even uglier. There was also violence at Port Vale, where an unprovoked attack on a small group of visiting QPR fans sparked all kinds of trouble.

A week later, the game witnessed an old fashioned 'end-taking' of the type not seen for decades, when fifty Rochdale fans infiltrated the home end at Halifax and kicked off five minutes into the game. Unfortunately for the home fans, the game had been designated as a 'police-free' fixture and so fighting continued for some considerable time before officers arrived to separate the factions.

The North of England saw more serious trouble the following weekend, first at Huddersfield and, more seriously, at Burnley. Sadly, the disturbances at the McAlpine Stadium, involving both Town fans and visiting Manchester City supporters, went on for several hours and received widespread coverage after an eight-year-old boy was punched and kicked, having been caught up in a disturbance while walking back to the town after the game. There was also fighting in the executive boxes inside the ground, which forced the police to close all the bars and eject a number of suited and booted individuals. In total, thirty-four people were arrested, of which thirty were from Manchester. Bizarrely, two of those detained were teenagers who were caught after allegedly breaking into a storeroom at the ground and stealing season tickets.

At Burnley, things were far more dangerous. It was widely reported that as many as 300 members of the Suicide Squad (possibly their biggest turnout for over ten years) and up to seventy Wigan supporters were involved in incidents that raged across the town throughout the day. Inevitably, the people who bore the brunt of the violence were the police, who at one point came under a sustained and vicious attack from the bulk of the local mob. In another incident, attempts were made to drag at least two policemen from their horses and it was even reported that individuals assaulted one horse and attempted to head-butt a police dog! By the end of the day, just nine arrests had been made, although police made it clear that they would scrutinise all available closed circuit TV (CCTV) footage to apprehend as many of those involved as possible.

One of the more bizarre incidents that month took place prior to the England versus Argentina friendly at Wembley on 23 February. A small group of Derby County fans had travelled down for the game and headed for Tottenham, where they entered a pub known to be a haunt of the local football lads. For whatever reason, things quickly got out of hand and spilled out into the street, where three of the Derby group sustained serious stab injuries to arms, back, neck and chest.

Just a few days later, English football was to witness something else it thought had been banished forever, when a game was held up due to fighting in the stands and the violence spilled over on to the pitch. The match was Wigan versus Stoke and the trouble inside the ground was allegedly caused by Wigan fans' refusal to honour a minute's silence for legendary Stoke and England player Sir Stanley Matthews, who had died the previous week. Whatever the truth of this, the fact is that Stoke supporters had arrived in Manchester in large numbers hours before the game and had clashed with both police and local fans long before they entered the stadium. Some estimates put the number of travelling fans as high as 400, and there were several arrests, as well as a number of injuries.

With Stoke already under the watchful eye of both the FA and the National Criminal Intelligence Service (NCIS), due to the increasing hooligan problem at the club, the incident received widespread media attention. Yet within days the English game suffered two far more serious knocks when supporters of two clubs became involved in serious disorder during trips to Europe.

The first of these was Chelsea, whose supporters headed for France and a Champions League tie in Marseille. The night before the game, seven supporters had been arrested after running battles had taken place on the Lyon Metro. Although all were released without charge the following morning, the pattern was set and more fighting broke out in Marseille in the hours leading up to the game. Later, inside the ground, matters quickly got out of hand when a group among the 2000 Chelsea supporters reacted angrily to missiles being thrown at them by the home fans. Things quickly deteriorated and the French riot police were forced to fire tear gas into the visiting fans to calm the situation down. More trouble erupted after the game as Chelsea fans ripped out seats and threw them at the home fans leaving the game.

UEFA launched an urgent enquiry, but even as the FA crossed its fingers and hoped for leniency, there was more bad press following Leeds' visit to Italy for a UEFA Cup tie against AS Roma.

The Yorkshire club was accompanied by upwards of 7000 supporters, including a sizable contingent from the Service Crew which was keen to test the local fans' reputation for being hard-core fighters. However, despite a few minor skirmishes in which small groups of Leeds fans were attacked, the locals refused to get involved in anything with the main firm, who had arrived outside the ground. Eventually, after the police had arrived, about 200 Italians began throwing missiles at the Leeds fans, who simply backed off to avoid arrest, but shortly after this episode, a small group of scarfers were set upon by an estimated hundred or so locals. During this incident, a father and his 16-year-old son received extensive stab wounds to their legs. Not surprisingly, the Leeds supporters were furious, especially when rumours began circulating that other Leeds fans had been slashed by knife-wielding youths riding past on mopeds.

Although in the days that followed it was widely acknowledged that the Leeds fans had been largely innocent victims, the fact that so many known hooligans had travelled and gone looking for trouble did not go unnoticed – not just by the authorities, but by the hooligan community, too. This was something that was to take on a degree of significance in the coming months.

With events in both France and Italy still fresh in the minds of the public, Stoke City hooligans hit the headlines once again when almost 350 of them wrecked a Hooters bar in the centre of Nottingham after their clubs game against Forest. The trouble, which required the presence of fire engines after someone set fire to some T-shirts, was interesting because coverage in the local media featured an apology from 'well-behaved' Stoke fans, who criticised the troublemakers for the shame they were bringing on the club and the city.

March saw another interesting incident when hooligans used a ferry in an effort to escape arrest. Violence occurred when Newcastle and Sunderland fans clashed outside the Porthole pub, overlooking the ferry landing at North Shields, and the two mobs fought a pitched battle with pool cues and batons. Two men were seriously injured – one with a fractured skull – and police arrested six at the scene. However, the bulk of the Sunderland mob was already sailing off into the distance, but, sadly for them, the police were waiting when their ferry docked and a further thirty were arrested.

The following weeks saw Arsenal fans involved in trouble in Hamburg ahead of the club's Champions League game against Werder Bremen, while there were also disturbances at games involving Watford, Huddersfield, Bury and Grimsby, and at the Oxford versus Reading derby.

In the following weeks there were also a number of bizarre and potentially dangerous occurrences involving rival groups. At Barnsley versus Manchester City fans stole a large number of police batons, while at Leicester City versus Manchester United fighting broke out in the ground between two groups of home fans simply because each believed the other to be United. Only when the police broke up the fighting did anyone realise what had gone on.

As the game moved into April, Balsall Heath in Birmingham witnessed fighting between upwards of a hundred City and Wolves fans, which not only featured the throwing of a petrol bomb, but reportedly had flares being fired at opposing fans! Tragically, one man was left with serious brain damage after the violence which spread to various areas of the city, and four policemen were hurt and at least five police vehicles badly damaged as well.

On the same day in Bristol, Stoke City goalkeeper Gavin Ward was attacked by two Rovers fans, who ran onto the pitch in injury time. The keeper had already been bombarded with missiles and play was held up for ten minutes while mounted policemen restored order behind the goal. Not surprisingly, with Euro 2000 looming and the English game still under intense scrutiny from both UEFA and the press, the incident received widespread coverage. The situation wasn't helped by the Stoke City manager screaming blue murder and demanding that his promotion-chasing side be awarded a 3–0 win and thus all three points, in accordance with an international rule which gives this as the standard punishment in the event of such an incident.

However, even before the dust had settled English football was dealt a far more terrible blow, the nature of which went way beyond anything we in this country had ever suffered before. Not for the first time it involved English football fans abroad being attacked with knives by local supporters. This time, though, instead of serious wounds we had deaths, two in fact – Chris Loftus and Kevin Speight, who were both from Leeds and both in Turkey for United's Champion's League tie against Istanbul side Galatasaray.

Much has been said about what happened on that fateful night, but in many people's opinion the most vivid and accurate account features in my book *Eurotrashed*. However, I take no credit for that, nor would I ever want any, because it was written by someone who was there, who saw first-hand what went on and who desperately wanted to set the record straight. My only contribution was a bit of editing and a platform, and I was only too happy to provide both. The plan was actually to include the entire thing here, for those who haven't read it, but for reasons of space it simply wasn't possible, so I would urge anyone to beg, borrow or even steal a copy of *Eurotrashed* to read what went on. It really was a horrific and wholly unnecessary tragedy.

The impact of the murders was immense, not least because the controversial decision was taken to play the game and Galatasaray took the win to move forward to the UEFA Cup final in Copenhagen, where, ironically, they would face another English club, Arsenal.

Inevitably, the authorities and an ever-hungry media focussed on the idea that Leeds fans would use the game in Denmark to extract revenge and that they would be aided by hard-core hooligans from just about every major club in Europe, almost all of whom had experienced the 'hospitality' of Turkish football first-hand. There were also concerns that the local Turkish immigrant population would side with the Turkish club and, as a consequence, would become involved in any trouble. These fears would turn out to be well founded.

Domestically, the trouble continued. The Bristol derby was marred by the wrecking of a pub during a fight involving over fifty rival fans, while Millwall's trip to Burnley was blighted by fighting before the game, during which thunderflashes and smoke canisters were hurled at police. Trouble continued inside the ground as fans of the London club attempted a pitch invasion, before ripping out seats and throwing them at police.

At the end of April, a massive police operation was put in place to prevent trouble at Stoke's home game against Cardiff. However, even before the match it was clear that the police had a battle on their hands as a group of 200 Cardiff fans wrecked buses taking them to the game and a mob of between 600 and 800 home supporters staged repeated ambushes on Welsh fans being escorted to the ground. Police even set up a search area to prevent weapons being taken into the stadium and the police presence was so heavy inside that at one stage a Cardiff player was prevented from taking a corner because a police horse was in his way.

Sadly, football was to suffer an even darker day just a week later, when a Swansea City supporter was crushed to death by a police horse at Rotherham during running battles before the Third Division championship decider between the two clubs.

With the potentially volatile UEFA Cup final fast approaching and Euro 2000 a matter of weeks away, the black cloud hanging over FA headquarters could be seen for miles. There were even those who voiced their feelings that the worst-case scenario of the national side being banned from the summer tournament was now a case of not 'if' but 'when'.

Come the week of the match in Denmark, stories began to circulate that small pockets of Arsenal fans had actually visited the city in the weeks prior to the game to familiarise themselves with the place and meet with local lads. True or not, the rumours succeeded in heightening what was already a tense situation and, as the fans began to arrive in the city, it quickly became clear that it was only a matter of time before things kicked off.

In the event, violence exploded the night before the game when a group of Arsenal fans were attacked outside a bar called Absalon. Despite being heavily outnumbered, the Arsenal fans managed to run the Turks, but not before one had received a serious stab wound. Almost immediately, more trouble broke out around the city and by the time the evening drew to a close, seven people had been badly injured and ten arrested.

The following morning, as news of the violence spread, Arsenal fans began gathering in bars around City Hall Square in the centre of the city. Fairly quickly, a group of Turkish fans began congregating on the other side of the square and, under the watchful and eager eyes of a large media pack, began goading the Englishmen. Soon after, missiles started being thrown and, with no police presence, the Arsenal fans decided enough was enough and steamed across the square. Despite being heavily outnumbered, and with more than a few Turks waving blades around, they dealt out a major kicking.

Inevitably, pictures of the fighting were soon being broad-cast across Europe. As a result, and in spite of the fact that in almost every incident the Arsenal fans had been either defending them-selves or reacting to intense provocation, English football took all the blame.

The media went into its usual frenzy, with the tabloids running story after story about the inevitability of trouble in the summer and the consequences that would have for our game. The police, mean-while, went into overdrive. A series of dawn raids removed numerous lads from circulation, while anyone appearing in court for anything remotely linked to football was handed a banning order. On top of that, a list of over a thousand names was passed to the Belgian and Dutch police, with promises that if any were spotted they would be lifted and either deported or jailed immediately – that's assuming they actually made it out of the country.

PR-wise, it appeared to be the last thing the game here needed, but among the hooligan community feelings were very different. Most simply took this as yet another sign that no matter what went on and where, if any English football fans were involved we would be blamed. But equally there was a collective sense of satisfaction that the Turkish fans had finally been taught a long overdue lesson.

Incredibly, despite the inevitable calls to pull the national side out of the tournament, UEFA was sufficiently impressed by the authorities' reaction to the trouble in Copenhagen to allow England and its army of fans to travel, albeit with yet another warning hanging over us. As it turned out, despite the best efforts of the media to stir things up, the tournament was relatively trouble-free. Indeed, there were only really two incidents worth mentioning.

The first took place in central Brussels the night before the game against Germany, when over 200 English lads kicked it off with some local Turkish immigrants. Unable to cope, the local police quickly summoned riot squads, which were forced to charge at the English and use tear gas to disperse them.

The second incident took place the next day in a small square in the centre of Charleroi. In short, what happened was that a few English lads got drunk and overreacted to the arrival of a group of mouthy Germans. That was it. No windows were broken, no one was seriously hurt and if you'd visited the square that afternoon you would hardly have known that anything had happened. However, if you'd looked at the media you would have thought World War Three had been and gone.

The problem was that from day one the England versus Germany clash had been tagged as the 'flash point' game and the Charles II Square had been picked out as the most likely location for any trouble. As a result, the world's media had set up shop at just about every vantage point overlooking the tiny square, while a small army of riot police were encamped in side streets, waiting and hoping for the call to action. Inevitably, when it came they went to town, first with riot police and then with both horses and water cannon, all of which combined to provide some quite incredible imagery, which an eager and salivating media flashed around the world.

To say it was an overreaction would be an understatement and it was made worse by the fact that in the surrounding twenty-four hours more than 850 people were detained by the police, the majority of whom were shipped back to England in a fleet of Belgian military aircraft.

Not for the first time, many of those deported claimed that the Belgian police's zero-tolerance tactic had simply been an excuse for them to use excessive force and make indiscriminate arrests. Tales of quiet bars and cafes being pepper-sprayed and any English inside being beaten and arrested were frequent, but once again, they fell on deaf ears. However, those who were there know the truth and that includes a number of English football liaison officers who, in some instances, actually took it upon themselves to warn lads to stay out of certain areas because the police were on the hunt.

Sadly, England were knocked out of the tournament early on and the fans returned home to more condemnation and yet more laws designed to deal with the violent minority. However, to many people who knew the score, the tournament had been a success. The widespread violence many had forecast simply hadn't materialised and instead the mood among the travelling barmy army had largely been one of passion, pride and enjoyment. On the international stage at least, the tide seemed to be turning. Sadly, that mood was not replicated at home.

Pre-season had already been tarnished by the now traditional summer trouble, the worst incident of which took place in Newport, when riot police were called to deal with violence that broke out inside Spytty Park involving home fans and those visiting from Cardiff City. But things really got going after the season proper began.

In early September, posters began appearing on walls around Swansea City's ground, the Vetch, which under the heading 'no runners' urged as many people as possible to travel by train to London for the forthcoming game against Millwall. On the day of the game, over 180 travelled and were involved in serious disorder before, during and after the game. At one point, the Welshmen used tear gas during confrontations with police at Paddington Station, forcing the London Underground to be shut down. Although accompanied by police on the trains back to Wales, more trouble erupted when a communication chord was pulled in Cardiff and efforts made to leave the train. Bizarrely, despite a day of trouble, only eight people were arrested, only one of whom was from Wales.

September also saw serious trouble at the Potteries derby, Chesterfield, Leicester and Manchester United, and Stoke versus Millwall, where police were forced to use tear gas to try and quell violence outside the ground after the game.

October saw Swansea City's increasingly notorious hooligan element involved in another major incident, this time on home territory. Ironically, the incident is best remembered for a frank and very public admission by the police that they had got their tactics for the game totally wrong.

They had been totally unprepared for the arrival of about 200 Bristol City fans in the city centre some four hours before kick-off time. Not surprisingly, trouble soon broke out and at least three pubs were wrecked and traffic in the city centre was brought to a standstill by battling fans before police, supplemented by officers hastily drafted in from all over the area, finally managed to get the situation under control. However, after the game, which had to be delayed for fifteen minutes due to the crowd trouble, more trouble broke out as police struggled to disperse the Bristol City fans and get them out of the city. At one point, Swansea fans emptied a skip full of rubbish to use the contents as missiles during a battle with the police. At least five officers were injured in the fighting and a police dog was blinded in one eye, yet there was not a single arrest.

Trouble returned to the European stage a week later when a Leeds United fan was stabbed in Italy ahead of the Yorkshire club's game against AC Milan. However, although trouble had been widely forecast, this was the only real incident of note, despite the fact that 5000–7000 Leeds fans had travelled to the game.

Just days later, two other Yorkshire clubs hit the headlines for very different reasons, when police were forced to use batons and tear gas to break up a group of 300 Wednesday and United fans after the Steel City derby. In all, thirty-three fans were arrested and the local MP made a very vocal and public appeal for them all to be given at least a three-year ban from all football grounds.

February 2001 saw Swansea City involved in yet more serious disorder when Millwall visited the Vetch. Ironically, the game was accompanied by the biggest ever anti-hooligan operation mounted in the city. This involved 350 policemen, including mounted officers from other forces, yet that didn't prevent trouble from breaking out when a group of a hundred local fans attempted to ambush a group of 400 Millwall fans being escorted to the ground from a special train. More violence erupted inside the ground when Millwall fans allegedly began throwing golf balls at the home supporters, forcing the game to be held up briefly. In all, twenty-two people were arrested, while the haul of weapons seized by the police included various knives, knuckle-dusters and even an axe! In spite of this, the police were quoted as claiming that their presence had prevented any serious disorder!

That same week, English fans were involved in another major incident abroad, but this time they were very much on the receiving end. The club in question was Liverpool, whose fans walked into what amounted to civil disorder when they travelled to Rome for a UEFA Cup tie. The previous weekend, an AS Roma fan had been thrown down some stairs by a policeman during a game at Bologna and was still in a coma. As a result, the crowd was in an angry mood and there was rioting before the game, forcing the police to take refuge inside the stadium. They were then attacked by fans already inside, so had to flee the stadium, leaving all their vehicles behind, and various cars, vans and motorbikes were torched.

Caught in the middle of this, five Liverpool fans received serious stab wounds and another three were put in hospital. Not for the first time, assistance for the injured fans from the authorities was negligible. As if to justify this, a British Embassy spokesman was quoted as saying: 'It sounds a bit drastic to say they were stabbed. The wounds were very superficial – they were barely punctures.'

At home, Millwall was involved in more trouble when the club's trip to Bristol City in March resulted in a semi-riot inside the ground, with seats being ripped up by both home and away fans. Afterwards, a group of around 200 Millwall fans battled with riot police as they tried to get at rival supporters without success.

With delicious irony, on the very same day the 30,000-member England fan club was disbanded in a move designed to re-launch the English support with a more positive and hooligan-free image.

Sadly, the bad news continued that same weekend when police were forced to baton-charge West Brom and Wolves fans after the Black Country derby at Molineux. A total of ten fans were arrested during and after the trouble, which the police accused the hooligans of arranging via mobile phones.

Two weeks later, the largest ever policing operation at a game in Lancashire, involving several hundred officers, failed to prevent serious disorder at Blackburn versus Burnley. The worst of the fighting took place in Accrington town centre after a large group of Blackburn fans had been ejected from the station, having been told they could not board a train. A standoff with police followed, during which an officer was dragged into a pub and suffered glass wounds to his face. In all, thirty-six people were arrested.

April saw yet more trouble involving Liverpool fans on their travels in Europe, when seven fans were arrested in Barcelona for an attack on two Spaniards ahead of the UEFA Cup semi-final.

May 2001 was tarnished by a show of force from Everton after the last game of the season at Goodison Park. Having played Sunderland in the afternoon, the bulk of their lads were reportedly drinking in pubs around the ground when news broke that Sunderland had remained in the city centre. The Everton mob immediately headed down there and serious disorder followed, involving upwards of 200 lads. Only the intervention of the police broke up the fighting, after which thirteen people were arrested and a sizable number ended up in hospital with cuts. Following this trouble, the remainder of the Everton lads headed for the main train station to confront Liverpool's lads returning from their game at Charlton. More disorder followed, with the Everton lads gaining a major result over their local rivals.

Hooliganism returned to the international arena in June when England travelled to Greece for a World Cup qualifier. Despite 450 known hooligans having been banned from travelling under the Football Disorder Act 2000, trouble broke out before the game, resulting in some seventy English fans being detained, although most were released shortly before the end of the game.

With no tournament in the summer, things appeared to settle down for a while, but if anyone had any preconceived notions that the 2001–02 season would be a calmer one on the hooligan front, then those ideas were shattered when Tottenham travelled to the New Den for a pre-season 'friendly' with Millwall and some of the most serious fighting ever seen in South London occurred.

It began around 11a.m., when around a hundred Millwall and a slightly larger number of Spurs fans clashed in Jamaica Road, Bermondsey. Only the intervention of the police drove the two groups apart, but the Millwall fans turned their attentions to them, pelting officers with missiles before entering the ground. Phone calls between the two groups led to the organisation of a further clash and both mobs began leaving the ground about ten minutes before the final whistle. However, by this time Millwall fans were already fighting the police in Ilderton Road and as more and more home fans joined this mob, eventually swelling it to almost 400, the police were forced to back off. At about the same time, the Spurs mob arrived and they, too, came under sustained attack, with fighting continuing at South Bermondsey Station. In all, thirty police officers and three horses were injured in the fighting, with one man receiving serious stab wounds.

The same month, Cardiff witnessed an evening of violence when local fans fought running battles with Manchester United supporters in town for the Charity Shield game against Liverpool the following day. Twenty-two people were arrested, including two youths aged eleven and thirteen, and a police officer suffered a broken arm. More trouble erupted ahead of the game at the Millennium Stadium the following day, when it was reported that local lads had joined up with Liverpool fans to attack the United supporters in Wood Street.

Millwall hit the headlines again on 18 August, when a massive police operation was put in place to prevent trouble at its game against Birmingham City. Although largely successful, there were attacks made by a sizable mob of home fans on the escort taking the Millwall fans back to New Street Station and further trouble broke out when Wolves supporters arrived at the station having travelled back from their game at Coventry.

The following week, the South East London club were at it again, this time on home turf. A mid-week visit from Cardiff for the first round of the Worthington Cup saw a relatively small group of fans travel from Wales, but Millwall fans ran riot in the streets outside, causing extensive damage to property, before turning their attentions on the police.

The police came under further attack from Millwall fans just four days later, when a mob of around 250 ambushed Burnley fans being escorted back to South Bermondsey. Trouble continued for almost an hour after the Burnley fans had left.

The next serious flash point came in September when England travelled to Munich for a game that was to go down in history as one of the great team performances. It also handed the German hooligans the chance to prove once and for all that they were capable of taking on the English, even if it was only on home soil. It was a chance they grabbed with both hands.

The first clashes came in Frankfurt on the Friday before the game when, despite a huge police presence, some 350 locals took over the subway and caused mayhem as they hunted for any English fans. In the event, there were only a few minor skirmishes and thirty-five Germans were arrested, but it certainly set the tone for the Saturday.

With almost 9000 English expected, including a sizable mob, despite yet another huge police operation the potential for trouble was immense. In the event, the German police did a reasonably efficient job of keeping the two groups apart, with most incidents taking place in the afternoon. The worst of these were at the café near the main railway station and in and around the Marienplatz in the city centre, where fans exchanged bottles and various other missiles. The most serious confrontation of all took place at a bar called the Augustiner, where fifty German and English fans clashed.

Despite this, the local police regarded the security surrounding the game as a success, with only 180 arrests, the bulk of which were German. The English police were not so thrilled, if only because increasing doubts were being cast on their ability to stop hooligans from travelling with the national side.

September was also marred by what was almost a terrible tragedy. On 22 September, Sheffield United fans returning from their game at the New Den met a large group of Manchester City hooligans who had been in the city for their game against Sheffield Wednesday. The two fought running battles in the city centre and at about 10p.m. serious trouble broke out at the train station. During this incident, four policemen were seriously injured and another almost died.

Police were also attacked at Coventry on the same day, when a group of 140 from Portsmouth's 657 Crew began dismantling the visitors' stand inside the Coventry ground. The second half was delayed until riot police brought the trouble under control, but further attacks on the police took place after the game and continued into the night.

The following month, the national side again hit the headlines when what police described as 'a gathering of some of England's worst hooligan groups' took place in Manchester on the night of England versus Greece. Not surprisingly, trouble soon broke out, with United and City fans clashing before the United mob became involved in an incident with Stoke City in Deansgate. There was also trouble involving Sheffield United and Oldham fans as skirmishes continued throughout the evening.

In October, Stoke City and Port Vale fans were in the news for all the wrong reasons when violence erupted at the Potteries derby. In all, eighty-four people were arrested during incidents which included a fight involving a hundred hooligans, some of whom were armed with iron bars and bricks. Trouble also occurred inside the ground, including a pitch invasion and a barrage of missiles being thrown on to the pitch.

It was also widely reported that a large group of Stoke fans were detained after the game en route to Cobridge, which had been the scene of serious race riots earlier in the year. The fact that sixty of these fans were detained for chanting racial abuse was clearly significant, but it had taken some 300 officers to control the supporters on what was a dark day for the city.

That same month, two Wolves fans were stabbed and five arrests made when Millwall headed for Wolverhampton and what police were certain was a pre-arranged fight between the two sets of fans. Police even claimed that a number of hooligans had arrived from London armed with baseball bats hidden under trench coats and knuckle-dusters with blades on the end.

Incredibly, in December 2001, more Liverpool fans were stabbed when the team returned to Roma for yet another encounter, this time in the Champions League. In a carbon copy of events just seven months before, the victims were merely people caught in the wrong place at the wrong time, rather than genuine hooligans, but yet again, little was done to provide either protection or condemnation of the Italians. More worryingly, the build up to the game saw the Liverpool supporters' coaches attacked with missiles as they approached the Stadio Olympico. There was also a repeat of the fighting between police and Roma fans that resulted in tear gas being used to quell trouble on the Curva Sud.

Millwall featured yet again in the record of shame when on 13 December their fans attacked a pub full of Portsmouth's 657 Crew near Waterloo station, on the morning of the teams' game at the New Den. The attack, which involved upwards of a hundred individuals and which police and locals claimed had been well organised, saw the Millwall fans attack the building, smashing every window in the process using pool balls. They then steamed into the pub, but Portsmouth fought back before police arrived. However, all those involved escaped before any arrests were made. After the game, more fighting broke out in the streets around the ground, this time involving almost 250 fans, yet only two arrests were made for public order offences.

Later that month, a group of approximately 300 Bristol City lads came under attack at Grangetown Station while being escorted to Cardiff City's ground, forcing police to baton-charge the local fans. During the game missiles, including bottles of urine, were thrown by the two groups and home fans fought with police for up to an hour after the final whistle.

Sadly, as the game moved into the new year and towards the 2002 World Cup in Japan and South Korea, things showed no signs of improvement. January saw organised serious trouble at Stoke City versus Everton, Liverpool versus Birmingham City, Aston Villa versus Manchester United, Chelsea versus West Ham, Chelsea versus Tottenham and Reading versus Oxford. There was also a major incident at Bolton versus Manchester United, where sixty riot police were deployed to keep rival fans apart in the town centre. The game also saw twenty arrests and a similar number of people were ejected from the ground during the game.

It was also widely reported that trouble which broke out at an Aberdeen versus Rangers game had been orchestrated by Chelsea and Tottenham lads who had travelled to Scotland to 'observe' how things happened north of the border. This was a story that caused great mirth among the English hooligan community, not least because it implied that the Scottish had little or no hooligan problem of their own and needed the English help to show them the way, which is just about as far away from the truth as it's possible to get!

However, the worst and most high-profile incident took place, once again, at Cardiff City, when the team's FA Cup tie against Leeds United was marred by the kind of disorder inside the ground that many thought had been eradicated. Violence outside the ground had created an already tense situation, but this was heightened when Leeds striker Alan Smith was sent off. Shortly afterwards, missiles began to be thrown at the Leeds fans, who quickly returned fire.

To make matters even worse, Cardiff chairman Sam Hammam went for a walk along the touchline and stood behind the goal his side were attacking, much to the anger of the Leeds United fans. At the final whistle, Cardiff supporters poured on to the pitch and began baiting the Leeds fans, but were kept back by police using dogs. Further clashes took place after the game with horses and dogs being used to control the rival fans. The FA was incensed and ordered Hammam to stop his habit of walking around during matches. It later emerged that the bodyguard who had accompanied him on his walk was a convicted hooligan who had only recently completed a twelve-month ban from all clubs in England and who was still high on the NCIS list of dangerous hooligans.

Another serious incident, albeit a slightly humorous one, hit the headlines in January when Millwall fans leaving the New Den after their game against Blackburn found an over-zealous clamper, who police later described as either the bravest or most stupid man alive, busily targeting a line of supporters' cars parked on a private estate. Not surprisingly, the mood soon turned ugly and the clamper's van was turned on its side before the police arrived and ordered him to release the vehicles without charge.

In February, police in Nottingham put in place an unprecedented operation employing 270 officers to keep Forest and Millwall fans apart. The operation, which involved closing thirty-six local pubs and moving the kick-off forward to midday, was almost a total success.

With the FA and the authorities now showing increasing concern at the likelihood of trouble in the Far East, the fact that the number of incidents of violence at games showed no signs of abating darkened the mood and the police crackdown began in earnest. Banning orders were handed out like confetti, but, interestingly, aside from the high-profile incidents, the police began refusing to release details of any trouble going on domestically, claiming that hooligans revelled in seeing their clubs feature in the press and such coverage encouraged them.

However, to many commentators the real truth of the matter was that things were getting out of control and the negative publicity could well have undermined the PR drive being mounted by the police and the FA to convince the host nation that the World Cup in Japan would be trouble-free, because they were on top of things. It was, not to put too fine a point on it, bullshit.

February saw more clashes and often these were both organised and vicious. Wigan, Blackburn, Oxford, Chester City and Shrewsbury Town all saw significant disorder, while riot police were deployed at Middlesbrough versus Leeds, Sheffield Wednesday versus Rotherham United and Sunderland versus Newcastle, where dogs and horses were injured during clashes in which thirty-eight fans were arrested.

Bizarrely, four Cardiff fans were arrested at Huddersfield, even though their game had been called off due to a waterlogged pitch! So concerned were police by the presence of the Soul Crew in the town that officers from four separate forces escorted their coaches down the M1 motorway and back towards Wales, with motorbike riders closing all exits as they passed.

March saw yet more trouble involving four clubs which were causing increasing concern to the authorities. Two of them, Millwall and Portsmouth, fought running battles around Fratton Park before and after their game, with riot police having to use batons to keep them apart. The South London club was also involved in serious disorder when some of its fans staged an attack on Sheffield Wednesday fans leaving the New Den. Cardiff City fans were involved in violence at Northampton and Chesterfield and there were also serious incidents at Tottenham versus Chelsea and Leeds versus Manchester United.

Not surprisingly, the trend continued in April. On 1 April, Grimsby and Sheffield Wednesday fans fought running battles in Cleethorpes and were only brought under control when police with dogs and horses were drafted in. Altogether, seventeen men were arrested.

Just four days later, 300 officers were deployed to keep order at the New Den when Wolverhampton Wanderers came to London intent on trouble. In the event, the police operation was a success, but not before Millwall fans had once again pelted the police with bricks, bottles and even fireworks.

Sheffield saw yet more clashes between fans in April, although in each instance these began with Wednesday and United fans confronting each other at the city's railway station. On the first occasion, 300 rival fans had to be kept apart as Wednesday headed for the teams' game at Stockport, while on the second, United supporters attacked Wolves fans arriving for their teams' game at Wednesday. The Wolves fans then came under attack from Wednesday supporters and after the game police were forced to deal with groups of hooligans from all three clubs roaming the city looking for trouble.

Before April drew to a close, among the usual litany of trouble there were three incidents which were significant, albeit for different reasons. The first involved Charlton and Southampton supporters who fought at Maze Hill railway station in South London. Although nothing major in hooligan terms, what marked this out as important is the way that this so-called 'Battle of Maze Hill' would later be used in dramatic fashion by both the police and the media.

The basic facts are that fifteen or so Southampton fans got off the train at Maze Hill to be met by twice the number of Charlton lads. Things kicked off immediately and lasted around two or three minutes, before the police arrived and the two groups did the off. However, with Japan on the horizon the police latched on to the incident and, using CCTV footage as well as mobile phone and computer records, managed to trace some of the men.

Two years later, just ahead of Portugal 2004, seventeen of those involved were brought to trial, yet what really captured the media attention was the fact that one of the men, a teacher, hadn't even been present at Maze Hill, but was nevertheless sentenced to two years for his role in organising the fight via the internet. Immediately, the press began talking about hooliganism's cyber subculture and the fact that this finally proved that football violence was indeed highly organised (sic). For the police, this was a huge PR coup. Not only did it prove that they were willing and able to do whatever it took to bring hooligans to justice, but the fact that Euro 2004 was so close allowed them to claim that all seventeen of the men imprisoned would have been heading for Portugal and so they had obviously removed a potential problem.

The second incident took place at Preston, when a local Asian man was attacked by a small group of football fans after his car had been involved in a minor accident. Shortly afterwards, a group of Asian men arrived on the scene, having been summoned by the driver, and the situation rapidly began to escalate into violence which lasted for over four hours before police brought things under control. Reporting of this event by both the police and the local media claimed it was a racially motivated event. However, according to those who were there this certainly wasn't the case, at least not initially, but that is how it ended up. Sadly, it wasn't the last such incident involving football fans as more and more of the organised groups began to respond to things that were going on the length and breadth of the country in the name of multiculturalism.

The final event of note in April 2002 was perhaps the most significant in terms of the impact it had on the game at the time. For months the papers had been filled with concerns about how English fans would behave at the forthcoming World Cup and those concerns were given fresh impetus when Manchester United headed for a Champions League semi-final against Leverkusen. This resulted in 128 people being detained, of which 123 were English.

Ironically, Liverpool fans had clashed with hooligans from the German club after losing their quarter-final tie a fortnight earlier, but police sources claimed that the events related to the Manchester United game were far more significant given the number of people involved and the severity of the violence.

The most serious incident surrounding this fixture took place in the centre of nearby Cologne, which was packed with revellers celebrating the German May Dance festival. Almost 300 fans had to be driven apart by police using baton charges and dogs. Much to the chagrin of the English police, the Germans refused to charge any of the English fans. Instead, they simply took their details, photographed them and then shipped them out. The move incensed the British Government, which was by now increasingly desperate for its much-lauded cross-border anti-hooligan initiative to become more than a pipe dream. That desperation intensified when the end-of-season play-offs were marred by two major incidents of trouble involving four clubs who had become synonymous with football hooliganism – Cardiff City, Millwall, Stoke City and Birmingham City.

On 1 May over 600 Cardiff fans attacked Stoke supporters as they were leaving Ninian Park, following the Welsh club's defeat. Not

KICKING OFF

surprisingly, Stoke responded and officers were forced to use batons to keep the two groups apart as missiles, including bricks and bottles, were thrown from among the Cardiff support.

The following day, South London experienced what was described as some of the worst violence seen on the streets of the capital in living memory when Millwall fans rioted after their club's play-off defeat to Birmingham City. At its height, almost a thousand Millwall fans spent over an hour hurling bricks and paving slabs at police, while weapons including flares, fireworks and even a chisel were used during the fighting. A number of cars were also set on fire.

So concerned were the police at the level of violence around the New Den that the Birmingham fans were kept locked inside the stadium, while it was over an hour before it was deemed safe enough for the Birmingham City players' coach to be escorted from the ground. Only the arrival of reinforcements, which swelled police numbers of over 200, managed to quell the trouble, which left forty-five officers injured, six of whom required hospital treatment for, among other things, a broken arm, a broken leg and a broken foot. Significantly, every member of a twenty-one strong tactical support group unit were injured, as were twenty-four out of thirty-six mounted policemen on duty. Three horses also suffered serious wounds, one of which almost proved fatal.

I have to say, footage of this incident is absolutely terrifying and one can only wonder what it must have been like to have been in the middle of it. Indeed, a documentary broadcast some time later included an interview with one of the policemen who had been responsible for filming the trouble and, despite the fact that some months had passed, the poor guy was almost in tears, such had been his fear on the night.

Interestingly, the usual post-mortem into the trouble included claims from furious senior police officers that the level of trouble was totally unacceptable and that they intended to sue Millwall Football Club for the cost of the operation and would be looking for compensation for officers injured on the night. However, this eventually came to nothing.

Sadly, this wasn't to be the last domestic hooliganism of the 2001–02 season, for both the division one play-off and the Welsh Cup final were marred by violence, but now all eyes were beginning to turn eastwards to the 2002 World Cup in Japan and Korea.

It is no exaggeration to say that the Japanese, force-fed by a crazed media with pictures of Millwall, Heysel and Marseille, genuinely believed that Armageddon in the shape of English football fans was on the way. As if to confirm this, anti-riot exercises were staged using locals dressed in England shirts and talk was of new technology such as net guns to fire at anyone who became involved in fighting. There were even companies making fortunes selling hooligan insurance to an eager public.

In England, the wave of banning orders reached four figures, while the media was going crazy about hooligans using false passports, organised mobs heading for Thailand and Australia, and even stories of Japanese gangs threatening to take on the English hooligans.

What no one realised, however, was that nothing was ever going to happen for one simple reason: even if there were lads travelling out looking for trouble, a claim which itself is debatable, there wasn't going to be anyone for them to fight with. Other European countries don't export their hooligans and South America doesn't either, but, more significantly, there is no culture of hooliganism in either Japan or South Korea. As a result, the tournament was a blast and the English will long be remembered not for the trouble they brought with them, but for their passion, noise and colour. Sadly, the good news wasn't to last for long.

CHAPTER TWO

2003 TO THE PRESENT

While the success of the tournament in the Far East had strengthened the notion that the continuing moves to change the image of the support surrounding the national side were paying real dividends, any hopes that this would be replicated on the domestic stage were dashed when the pre-season friendlies began just a few short weeks later.

Around 3000 Manchester City fans travelled to Hamburg with their side and the night before the game trouble erupted in the city's red-light district. There were more incidents during and after the game and these saw forty-six people arrested, although most were German.

Three days later, Everton fans were involved in a series of disturbances in Belgium when the team travelled to Anderlecht. However, in this instance they were certainly on the receiving end of some horrific policing methods, which included women, children and even in one instance a disabled youngster being sprayed with tear gas and water cannon. It was a disgraceful exhibition of police brutality, yet, once again, it received no condemnation by the English authorities, which, given the circumstances, was equally shameful.

Arsenal fans were also present, although none were involved, when trouble erupted among home fans when they visited Austria for a game against Rapid Vienna. So bad did the fighting and missile-throwing become that players were forced to flee rioting fans and, although an attempt was made to restart the game, it was eventually abandoned altogether.

The 2002–03 season proper saw the usual trouble on opening day and this continued over the following weeks, most notably at Plymouth, where the game with Bristol City saw police forced to baton charge rival fans in the city centre.

However, in September the problem of football violence once again hit the national headlines, and in the worst possible way, when Watford played host to their near neighbours L*t*n for a Worthington Cup tie.

Despite a huge police presence, a large contingent of L*t*n supporters arrived in the town mid-afternoon and trouble started shortly afterwards, with the most serious incident being at the Moon under the Water pub in the high street. However, as kick-off time approached and with the players already on the pitch warming up, disorder broke out in Occupation Road adjacent to the ground. Even as police were struggling to keep the two sets of fans apart outside, about fifty L*t*n fans already inside the stadium pushed their way past stewards and made their way on to the pitch.

For a few minutes they goaded the home support in the Lower Rouse stand and, with no police presence to stop it and the players being urged to return to the dressing rooms, violence soon erupted. In spite of the fact that the Lower Rouse is home to mainly families and children, a few individuals from among the home support leapt on to the pitch and fought back, before the police finally appeared and, after ten minutes, managed to force the fans back into the stands, leaving two seriously injured with head wounds.

Unfortunately, the game was being broadcast live on television and the cameras captured every detail of the violence. This footage was to form an integral part of the evidence which the police would present to the courts over a year later and resulted in twenty men being sentenced to a total of eighteen years in prison, with all of them being banned from games for a combined total of 143 years.

September also saw Stoke City fans return to the list of shame, but not simply for the usual reasons. A police operation involving 250 officers and costing in excess of £50,000 was employed to stop Stoke clashing with rival fans when the Midlands club headed for Burnley.

However, it later emerged that one of the primary reasons for the scale of the operation was in response to intelligence suggesting that a section of the City support were planning to link up with far-right extremists who had arrived in the region with the aim of stirring up racial tension in Burnley, a town which had witnessed a number of serious racially motivated incidents in the months prior to the game.

In the event, the operation was a success, with arrests limited to the usual football-related violence. However, Stoke's increasingly bad reputation was causing severe concern to the authorities. It was also cementing their place at the top of the hooligan tree.

A club rarely remarked upon in hooligan circles featured towards the end of the month when trouble broke out among supporters during Fulham's trip to Croatia for a UEFA Cup tie with Hajduk Split. A small group from the West London club fought with local hooligans, but came badly unstuck, leaving some badly injured.

Back at home, pitch invasions hit the headlines first at Birmingham, where a fan confronted Aston Villa goalkeeper Peter Enkelman, and then at Wrexham, where trouble broke out among Everton fans, forcing the referee to suspend the game for several minutes. Nine people were arrested during the incident, which was broadcast on television.

October saw a sad return to trouble involving England fans when violence broke out during a European Championship qualifier in Bratislava, a game marred by some quite horrific racist abuse hurled at Emile Heskey and Ashley Cole by the home supporters. With tension already high as a result of an incident the previous night, when two England fans received gunshot wounds after security guards fired sixteen shots at a group who refused to leave a bar in Bratislava, and the arrival of riot police who wore not only the usual helmets and armour but balaclavas and uniforms with no markings to hide their identities, it didn't take long before things turned ugly.

First missiles were exchanged and then, following a Slovakian goal, England supporters charged at a fence separating them from the celebrating home fans. Shortly afterwards, as some of the crowd began ripping out seats, the riot police waded in and unleashed some quite horrific treatment on the visitors. Some England fans have claimed that their behaviour was a reaction to the missiles being thrown at them by the Slovakians and that the charge was as a direct result of the racist abuse directed at the two England players. If this is true it would be ironic, given the history of a section of English fans. However, although initially supported by the FA, the very idea was ridiculed by certain sections of the English media. UEFA wasn't thrilled either. It charged the Slovakian authorities for the racist abuse and the FA over the conduct of the England fans.

The month was to see further trouble domestically with riot police having to keep Stoke City fans (again) apart from visiting Wolves supporters during their televised game at the Britannia Stadium. Trouble had actually started some hours before the game, when two mobs clashed in Stafford some twelve miles away and at least eighteen fans were being held in custody even before the kick-off.

Sadly, November was no better. If anything, it was even worse. Before the month was even half-way through Northampton, Oxford and Sheffield United versus Leeds United all saw major disorder, the latter being particularly nasty as it involved a pitch invasion and trouble in the city centre before and after the game. There were also incidents before and after the Manchester derby.

On 12 November, Liverpool, desperately needing a win to progress in the Champions League, headed for Basle, accompanied by legions of fans, including an estimated thousand or so without tickets. The local lads had been steadily building their own hooligan reputation, so it came as no surprise that a clash occurred on the night before the game. What was surprising was that it happened in Zurich, over a hundred kilometres from Basle, and that the bulk of the 'local' support were in fact German.

Although much of the trouble occurred around the main railway station, the incident that received the most publicity happened at a McDonald's burger bar, when a small group of Liverpool fans found themselves confronted by a mob of some forty to fifty locals. Having backed into the restaurant and kept the Basle fans at bay by throwing chairs at them, the Liverpool supporters were stunned when a petrol bomb exploded in the doorway, meaning that no one could get in or out. Thankfully, it wasn't life-threatening, but by the time the police arrived the bulk of the Basle group had left and so, inevitably, the English fans took the brunt of their anger, despite only three of the fifteen people arrested being from Liverpool. There were yet more clashes on the day of the match that resulted in over forty arrests for vandalism and disorder.

In many ways, 2003 was a significant year for hooliganism as the police, helped by better intelligence and increasingly draconian legislation, in particular the banning order scheme, began to clamp down ever harder on the travelling groups. However, as the month of January progressed, this did not prevent serious trouble occurring at numerous games, including the Sheffield derby, Arsenal versus Oxford and Aston Villa versus Blackburn. Cardiff also became embroiled in a number of confrontations with the increasingly notorious West Yorkshire police during a trip to Huddersfield. In what was proving to be a familiar and aggressive style of policing, the Welshmen were given short shrift by officers, many of whom wore balaclavas and allegedly had their numbers hidden to avoid identification.

Manchester United also hit the headlines, first when a mob of 300 West Ham fans landed on their doorstep and then in February when they became involved in major disorder in Birmingham ahead of the game against City.

Just a few weeks later, they were at it again. This time in Bolton, when their fans became involved in a massive battle at Bolton railway station. The trouble occurred when a group of some hundred home supporters confronted sixty-plus United lads who were about to leave for Manchester after the game. Twelve people were arrested during the fighting, which left one man struggling for his life.

Birmingham was the scene of more trouble when violence erupted during City's derby game against local rivals Aston Villa at Villa Park. Trouble had flared before the game, but the real problems began inside the ground as, in almost a repeat of the previous game, when a fan had taunted Villa keeper Peter Enkelman, Birmingham midfielder Robbie Savage was confronted by a fan on the pitch, while officers from among almost 300 on duty at the match battled to stop Villa fans getting at City supporters located in the Doug Ellis stand. Fighting continued after the game and, in all, almost forty supporters were arrested and two policemen injured.

The next major flash point came at the end of March when England fans travelled to Zurich for the national side's Euro 2004 qualifier against

Liechtenstein. The night before the game twenty-five individuals were arrested during clashes in and around the city centre, with one fan being taken to hospital after police fired tear gas and rubber bullets to quell the trouble. The following day, more trouble broke out, during which ten English fans were arrested and five seriously wounded, three suffering gunshot wounds and two serious stab wounds. English police later claimed that the trouble had been caused by groups of foreign hooligans, although no one seemed able to actually prove this.

The following week, the England fans were again in trouble, this time when Turkey headed for Sunderland and their Euro 2004 qualifier with England. Tempers were already running high following the murders of two Leeds United fans in April 2000 and further trouble in Copenhagen ahead of the UEFA Cup final the same season. There were also very real concerns that the situation in Northern Iraq would result in increased tensions between the Kurdish and Turkish communities in the North East, which were already running high following the murder of an Iranian asylum seeker.

To counter these concerns and to head off any potential trouble, the police staged one of the largest operations ever seen at a game in the North East, with over a thousand officers on duty. As a result, there were no major disturbances involving Turkish fans, although it wasn't for want of trying, with a large number of English lads battling with police as they attempted to get at the visiting support, something only officers using batons and dogs were able to prevent. However, this wasn't the most significant incident on the night. That involved groups of Sunderland and Newcastle fans who fought a pitched battle among themselves.

By the time the evening had drawn to a close, ninety-five people had been arrested, but of more concern to the authorities was the fact that due to the nature of some of the chanting, the trouble was being perceived as being racially motivated, which simply wasn't the case. It was, instead, nothing more than the desire of the English hooligan community to extract revenge for events in Istanbul.

Just days after the problems at Sunderland, the *People* newspaper ran one of those unintentionally hilarious stories about hooliganism and the people involved in it. Under the headline 'Soccer riot cops hunt "Burberry Boys" gang' it explained that the thugs behind the riot in the North East were some of the game's most notorious hooligans, who identified themselves by wearing Burberry baseball caps. Furthermore, the gang were being targeted by undercover officers who were determined to smash them once and for all. It was completely ridiculous and did nothing to enhance the image of the paper. However, events at Sunderland did have a major and far more real impact on the English game.

Even before the dust had settled, UEFA had launched an urgent enquiry and almost immediately concerns were voiced that, because of the nature of the charges, England would have to play their next home qualifier behind closed doors. This assumption was based on the fact that, following the game in Bratislava, the FA had fought long, hard and ultimately successfully to force UEFA to impose such a penalty on the Slovenian game.

However, desperate for the income a full house at Middlesbrough would provide, the FA began some serious lobbying, part of which allegedly included an offer to refuse its ticket allocation for the game in Turkey, a match that was already causing the authorities sleepless nights. True or not, in the event UEFA imposed a fine of 150,000 Swiss francs (£75,000) on the English game – the largest sum it had ever imposed for a racism-related offence – but allowed the game against Slovenia to go ahead in front of the English support.

With the game in Turkey fast approaching, the concerns which for years had been part and parcel of any trip involving the national side took on increasing significance to everyone involved with the hooligan issue. Events in Istanbul were still fresh in the memory of many and there were very real fears that lives would be lost if fans travelled to Istanbul and became involved in trouble. UEFA also made it clear that should anything happen, no matter what the result, England and its travelling fans wouldn't be going anywhere near Portugal.

For once, just about everyone saw sense, including a number of lads who made the conscious decision to withdraw from active participation for fear of attracting a banning order and missing out on a summer in the sunshine. However, in many instances that wasn't enough. In August, shortly before the game against Liechtenstein at Old Trafford, police sent more than 170 letters to known hooligans warning them to stay away.

The letters, which read, 'If you travel to, or are sighted in Manchester city centre, or the vicinity of Old Trafford football ground, it may be interpreted as an attempt to become involved in football-related disorder and police action will be taken against you,' gave as stark a warning as it were possible to give. However, although the game passed by peacefully, it also showed increasing nervousness on the part of the authorities, who were still reeling from having to announce a nineteen per cent increase in arrests the previous season.

Interestingly, the police blamed this increase on a 'new generation' of young hooligans, the majority of whom were not known to them. Yet incredibly, while the annual report claimed a huge success in the number of games which had occurred without incident or arrest (thirty-seven per cent of Premiership matches, seventy-one per cent of First Division games and eighty per cent in the Second Division), it avoided stating that the main reason these figures were so high was simply because the police weren't arresting anyone on the ground anymore. Rather, they were employing CCTV to obtain convictions later on.

A perfect example of this came just days after the England game at Old Trafford, when Sheffield United and Cardiff City, two of the clubs who had made significant contributions to that increase, met at Bramall Lane. Intelligence had warned that a large element of the Soul Crew planned to arrive in Sheffield in the morning to kick things off early with their hosts and this proved to be accurate. However, despite a huge operation, clashes described by a senior officer as some of the worst seen in South Yorkshire for years delayed the kick-off for some ten minutes. In spite of this, there were just six arrests.

In September, increasingly fearful of crowd trouble which might result in the side being banned from Euro 2004, the FA decided to try and deter fans from travelling to Eastern Europe by announcing that they were handing their entire ticket allocation for the game against Macedonia to local disadvantaged children.

Furthermore, due to the concerns about the game in Turkey, they finally admitted what people had long since suspected – that no tickets for the game in Istanbul would be sold to England fans and that everything possible would be done to try and deter people from travelling to the Sukru Saracoglu stadium.

It was a bold idea, but it was badly flawed, for there had always been those who travelled independently and purchased tickets from touts near the ground and all this did was encourage more people to follow that path. In Macedonia this led to almost 500 England fans being dotted around the stadium in small groups and at the mercy of local hooligans and the 1800 riot police on duty.

Thankfully, other than the now seemingly inevitable racial abuse aimed at England players when in Eastern Europe, there was no serious trouble, but in the days that followed the players came in for criticism after acknowledging the travelling support following the 2–1 victory. After all, they shouldn't even have been there and with the FA desperate to stop fans travelling to Turkey, fears were that this would be perceived as encouragement to make the trip. To add further fuel to the fire, the head of the Turkish FA came out and said that if the England fans wanted tickets, they would be able to buy them on the night.

In the event, despite the importance of the game and the threats that had been flying around in both the media and on various hooligan-related message boards, only a handful of English fans made it to Istanbul and the game passed by without incident.

As a consequence, and with the team having secured the result they needed, England had made it through to the tournament and would be heading to Portugal for a month of sun, sea, beer and football. You could almost hear the groans coming from certain quarters and things weren't made any easier when, in mid-October, eighty-seven Newcastle fans were arrested during the club's trip to NAC Breda for a UEFA cup tie.

The worst trouble took place the night before the game when Newcastle supporters became involved in a number of small skirmishes and then clashed with 200 Dutch riot police who had been deployed to bring things under control. Somewhat bizarrely, rumours were rife among the Newcastle support that much of the trouble was started by Feyenoord fans who had travelled to Breda seeking revenge for Newcastle knocking them out of the Champions League the previous season. There were also claims that a small number of Chelsea fans were involved, although no one has ever been able to confirm this.

Already furious, the English authorities were incensed when the

Dutch released all the Newcastle fans and let it be known that none would face any charges in Holland, although they were speaking to Northumbria police. Once again, the idea of cross-border co-operation had been dashed – the last thing they needed with Portugal now firmly inked on to the calendar and the problems it might bring.

However, while all eyes were beginning to turn towards the summer, domestically things continued along the usual rocky path. One of the more interesting incidents took place in Birmingham where a group of some 150 Zulus chased Villa fans all over the city centre, even smashing shop windows at one point as they battled to get at their rivals who had fled inside. Riot police eventually arrived and drove the Birmingham fans out of the centre, but a small group broke off and returned, fighting a second battle with their near neighbours before fleeing when the police managed to track them down for a second time.

Three days after this incident, Manchester United fans were arrested when a mini-riot marred the Champions League tie against Rangers in Glasgow. Twenty-five were detained during disturbances before the showpiece 'Battle of Britain' game at Ibrox, as fighting broke out in Paisley Road. A further twenty-four were arrested during the game and a single arrest was made afterwards. United fans were kept inside the ground for over an hour after the game to allow police to disperse the Rangers support.

A week later, the English game saw an incident which has settled into hooligan folk law as one of the most audacious attacks staged by an organised group in recent years. Ironically, it received little or no coverage in the national press, largely because it was simply so, well, unbelievable. The mob concerned were West Ham and their targets, their old sparring partners at White Hart Lane. With the game a mid-week Carling Cup tie, the evening kick-off gave the East London firm plenty of time to sort themselves out and around lunchtime a large group headed off across London with the aim of hitting Spurs at the Cockrell pub in Tottenham High Road.

Incredibly, the mob made it all the way across London undetected and arrived at White Hart Lane station with over eighty lads. Having left the station, they were spotted by a small group of Spurs fans, but although half the West Ham mob gave chase, the local lads fled. This now meant that West Ham had two groups of forty lads, both of which headed toward the Cockrell.

As the first group approached the pub, a mob of between thirty-five to forty-five Tottenham fans came pouring out of a side entrance and launched a barrage of missiles at the attackers. This stopped West Ham in their tracks and they even backed off a bit, but, just as the ammunition ran out, the second group of West Ham arrived and together they charged, forcing the Tottenham lads to turn and run. Half of them made it back into the pub, slamming the doors behind them, but in doing so they trapped their mates outside. These fled up the High Road.

The West Ham mob then set about trying to force open the doors which, given that the Cockrell is a former bank, was a wasted effort. They then laid siege to the windows, but these were also reinforced and so, with no way in, they backed off.

At this point, the police finally arrived in the shape of two female officers and so West Ham headed off towards Northumberland Park where the Tactical Support Group (TSG) finally got hold of them and arrested seventy-eight individuals. This was not, however, the total number involved, for a good many lads managed to slip away as soon as the TSG appeared. More skirmishes took place throughout the evening, with at least two further pubs damaged. The final arrest total was ninety-three, the bulk of which were West Ham.

Whichever way you look at it, this was a major result for West Ham against their local and bitter rivals. However, questions remained as to how such a large group were able to travel right across London without attracting attention from either the Metropolitan or British Transport police. There were even suggestions that the whole thing had been set up by the police in an attempt to gain sufficient evidence to smash the Inter City Firm once and for all. However, despite the large number of arrests, only a very few were ever convicted. If nothing else, this highlighted the problems the police were having domestically, but equally it showed just how difficult a job they faced in the coming months, not just in London, but across the country. For once, it was a challenge they were happy to rise to.

Indeed, from this point on all eyes turned to Portugal and the forthcoming European Championships. Optimism was rife that the team would finally realise its potential and the mood among the travelling England support was extremely positive on the back of the success in Japan. Equally, the banning order system was proving increasingly effective, with police adopting a 'keep the problem in this country' approach and claiming that the 1800 orders already in place would be supplemented by at least a further 500 come the start of the tournament. At one stage there were twenty-eight separate forces conducting anti-hooligan operations targeting sixty-six clubs and over 600 specific targets.

Even the Portuguese police remained quietly confident that the 50,000 Englishmen they expected to arrive on their doorstep in the summer would be largely well-behaved. However, that didn't stop them spending almost 17 million Euros on the security operation, which included, among other things, 150 new police cars and a few water cannon, the first ever seen in Portugal.

In February 2004, England travelled to Portugal for a friendly which was seen largely as a test of the security operation set-up for the summer. Thankfully, the game passed by without trouble and police in both countries deemed the operation a huge success, with twenty known hooligans being detained at airports in the UK as they attempted to leave England.

Yet even as the mood of optimism filtered through the game, trouble erupted at Upton Park when West Ham fans clashed with Cardiff City supporters as the Welsh club descended on East London for the first time in twenty-four years. Fighting took place throughout the day with the worst incidents afterwards, most notably in the Barking Road, which at one point was supposedly littered with battered bodies.

The same day, seventy-four Hull City fans were detained after wrecking a hotel the night before their game with Lincoln City, and in Bristol a huge battle broke out involving fans from four different clubs.

With Middlesbrough and Bolton already drinking in the city ahead of the Carling Cup final the following day, the arrival of Bristol City, returning from their game at Sheffield, where they had already been involved in a pre-arranged fight with Sheffield Wednesday fans, and a small number of Cardiff fans returning from the trouble at West Ham made violence inevitable and it exploded in the waterfront area. Police were forced to use tear gas and draw batons to disperse fighting fans, but the violence continued. At least one bar was wrecked and police had to evacuate a number of pubs in the city centre after telling them they had to close. Despite the severity of the trouble and the number of people involved, police made just six arrests.

Later that month, Portsmouth and Southampton fans were involved in serious disorder, despite an operation involving 400 officers, but the real trouble that day came back in London.

Millwall versus West Ham was always going to be a major problem for the police and so to combat the threat of violence, they put together the largest security operation ever seen for a game in the history of British football. There were 1100 officers on duty at a cost of over £270,000, but violence broke out inside the New Den when West Ham goalkeeper Stephen Bywater was sent off fifteen minutes into the second half. A group of 200 West Ham fans tried to force their way through a security cordon to get at the Millwall support and only the intervention of riot police and eight mounted officers on the pitch managed to bring things back under control. It was a shameful episode and pictures were sent across Europe – the very last thing the game needed with so much at stake ahead of the summer tournament.

However, the next test for the police was a huge success, because as England fans headed to Gothenburg for a friendly with Sweden, operations at airports the length and breadth of the country netted numerous known and suspected hooligans. As a result, the game was trouble-free, lending further weight to the idea that, on the international scene at least, things had finally changed.

From that point on it was all about dawn raids and banning orders. Magistrates began throwing them around like confetti to anyone who stepped out of line, no matter what club they followed, with the number increasing twenty-five-fold compared to Euro 2000. Among those hauled into court were lads from Derby, Coventry, Stoke, Burnley, Plymouth and Leicester, while the release of the controversial movie *The Football Factory* caused uproar in the popular press, with all and sundry criticising the producers for its timing.

Ironically, Millwall, one of the clubs featured in the film, had somehow made it to the FA Cup final against Manchester United and although the papers were full of doom and gloom, including reports claiming that hooligans from the two Bristol clubs had linked up to take on anyone stopping in the town on the weekend of the final, the game passed by relatively smoothly, with only two football-related arrests.

The police and the authorities breathed a collective sigh of relief and turned their weary eyes towards Portugal. The sheer scale of the operation to prevent trouble at Euro 2004 was breathtaking, not only here, but in the host nation. Aside from the 2700 banning orders that had already been put in place, legislation had given the police the power to intercept and stop anyone they suspected might be potential troublemakers from leaving the country. There were also record numbers of English 'spotters' going to the tournament, while the Portuguese had reintroduced specific border controls, which allowed them to stop and detain anyone they didn't want in their country.

Incredibly, it worked and in the main the mood among the England fans was jovial and friendly. However, it wasn't all sweetness and light. There was serious disorder on the Algarve with riot police having to control up to 400 drunken Englishmen in Albufeira. Thankfully, most people realised that the bulk of those involved were not football hooligans in the true sense of the word, but merely Englishmen who were using the tournament as an excuse to get drunk and play up on their holidays. Few had tickets for games, even fewer had any intention of travelling to where England was playing and not even UEFA believed that the FA could be held responsible for them.

Sadly but inevitably, defeat to the host nation in the quarter-finals saw the fans heading home, but for once they returned with their heads held high. With a few exceptions, they had done themselves and their country proud and for once they received glowing praise from UEFA.

The same could not be said of those watching the tournament here, because, with delicious irony, the worst trouble witnessed as a result of the tournament took place back in England. For example, forty riot police and dog handlers battled to control hooligans in the centre of Birmingham after the defeat to France and there was a total of eighty-three football-related arrests that same night across the country.

On the evening of England's defeat to Portugal, police in Jersey were forced to break up a mini-riot involving over 1400 people as disappointed locals turned their anger on each other. In Norfolk, a pub run by a Portuguese couple came under attack, while Exeter, Watford and Croydon also saw trouble as people struggled to keep their emotions in check. The latter incident was particularly violent with upwards of seventy people vandalising shops and restaurants and leaving scores of policemen injured.

However, with the game now in generally buoyant mood, albeit on the back of a huge and extremely expensive police operation, football began to look forward to a new and hopefully less violent future. Not for the first time, those hopes were dashed fairly rapidly.

In July 2004, Leeds travelled to Edinburgh for a pre-season friendly with Hibs and with them went a 300-strong mob from the notorious Service Crew. The Yorkshire fans caused trouble all weekend with the main flash point being the London Road.

In August, hooligans from West Brom and Aston Villa fought running battles along Oxhill Road, with over fifty becoming involved in a fight using baseball bats outside the Oakland pub in Handsworth. It took twenty riot police to bring the trouble under control and twelve men were arrested.

In September, English clubs were involved in various incidents during trips to UEFA Cup games. First, hooligans from Czech side Banik Ostrava fought running battles with Middlesbrough fans shortly before the sides took to the field, while in Hungary, Millwall fans became involved in all kinds of trouble ahead of their first ever European game. Bizarrely, a number of old heads from the South London club heaped praise on the Ferencvaros fans, claiming that they were among the best fighters they had ever encountered.

Just a month later, Millwall featured again, only this time, the club's fans were on the receiving end of violence which marred the Carling Cup tie against Liverpool at the New Den. The problems allegedly began when the home fans began hurling abuse, including references to the ninety-six people who died at Hillsborough. This obviously incensed the Liverpool fans who began ripping out seats and throwing them at the Millwall supporters, an action which only stopped when riot police came into the ground to prevent further disorder.

Six people were eventually jailed for their part in the trouble, with

others being banned from Anfield for three year
of this incident, Millwall found itself in the doch
fact that all the damage was caused in the sec
holding the Liverpool fans and that all those
Merseyside, Millwall fans were somehow for
chanting, while the Anfield club escaped seemii
trouble its fans had caused.

October also saw further trouble involving West Ham and Cardiff fans, although this time the circumstances were somewhat unique. When Cardiff travelled to Bournemouth for a Coca-Cola Cup tie, the last thing they expected to encounter was a coach-load of fans from East London, yet that is exactly what happened.

Posing as ordinary customers, the West Ham fans were drinking quietly, but a chorus of their trademark anthem 'I'm forever blowing bubbles' saw them launch into a ferocious attack on Cardiff fans drinking in the same bar, which left one man with a shattered jaw after being hit with a brick. It is claimed that this well-organised attack was in revenge for the Welsh fans' behaviour at Upton Park the previous February and that it had taken place in Bournemouth simply to avoid any police interference.

Later the same month the East Londoners were involved in trouble at Stamford Bridge when Mateja Kezman, the scorer of Chelsea's winning goal, was hit on the head by a missile. Coins and a plastic bottle were also thrown at other Chelsea players before riot police were forced to confront West Ham supporters located in the Matthew Harding stand. In all, eleven people were arrested for trouble both inside and outside the ground.

The next major incident took place at Elland Road in January where Cardiff City's Soul Crew clashed with police after being locked inside the ground following the match to allow the home fans to be dispersed.

Violence broke out once they were allowed out, leaving two officers with serious injuries. However, further clashes involving both sets of fans and police resulted in a series of dawn raids being staged in May, during which twelve men were arrested and charged with public order offences. One was actually detained at Pontefract hospital as his wife was waiting to give birth, while yet more were arrested after the local printed twenty-one pictures of those involved in the incident on the front page and asked readers to identify them!

Although never the most acceptable of activities, it had long been understood, even among the tabloid hacks, that hooliganism did involve a code of conduct of sorts and that there were lines over which the vast majority of lads refused to step. Sadly, March was to see two incidents which crossed the boundaries of 'acceptable', although to be fair they both received widespread condemnation from within the hooligan community. Indeed, one could argue that neither was actually hooligan-related at all, although both were treated as such by the police.

The first involved an incident that had taken place in Leicester Square in London's West End the previous October. Police had been on the trail of a group of Wolves fans since the incident in which four men, none of whom were football hooligans, had been viciously assaulted. A number had already been arrested during a series of dawn raids, but more were detained during Wolves' visit to Derby. Among them was a thirty-six-year-old woman and although she refuted the allegations and vowed to clear her name, there were suggestions that she had actually goaded the Wolves fans into the attack, which, if true, and given that she was actually a district nurse, was quite despicable.

The second incident followed Chelsea's Champions League defeat to Barcelona. With just about everyone involved with the West London club blaming referee Anders Frisk for the defeat, various websites soon became littered with abuse and then death threats. Eventually, Frisk's email addresses and even phone numbers appeared on the web and so bad and personal did the attacks become that Frisk decided enough was enough and retied from the game. It was a shameful episode and UEFA were furious. Chelsea coach Jose Mourinho was even called 'the enemy of football' by one official.

'Normal' service was resumed just a week later when trouble flared at the Merseyside derby. During the fighting, much of which took place after the game in the city centre, thirty-three people were arrested, most for public order offences. A police horse also suffered a serious slash to its hindquarters.

Trouble also erupted at the second city derby where a mob of almost 200 fought near a Mercedes dealership in Lichfield Road, Aston.

Hooligans rampaged through the streets hurling pool balls and bottles at each other before police swooped and arrested sixteen lads some five hours after the game at Villa Park.

The very next day, in what was becoming an increasingly familiar pattern, dawn raids hit the headlines again when twenty-six people were arrested across the country in connection with violence at Old Trafford, which had occurred ahead of England's game with Wales the previous October. The raids were timed to coincide with the build up to Northern Ireland's visit to Old Trafford and send a message to anyone looking to cause trouble that they weren't welcome. However, just to make sure that the message reached the right people, the football banning authority sent 2800 letters to known football hooligans warning them to stay away. A further hundred letters were sent by Greater Manchester police to individuals deemed to be 'high risk', warning them not to even enter the city centre on the day of the match. Thankfully, the game was trouble-free.

April saw hooliganism return to the European stage when Liverpool fans were subjected to a barrage of sustained hatred by Juventus fans during their Champions League visit to Turin.

Efforts to rebuild bridges destroyed by the Heysel tragedy in 1985 apparently came to nothing as the local Ultra groups hurled missiles, seats and flares at fans from the Merseyside club. Only the intervention of riot police managed to prevent violence, although prior to the game there had been a small number of incidents, including an attack on Liverpool fans by a group of masked men wielding various weapons, among them an iron bar.

Domestically, trouble continued throughout the month with the worst incident taking place in Bristol on St George's day, after Rovers' clash with Swansea City. With the Welsh supporters already being escorted back along the M4 towards the border, fighting broke out among two groups of local fans, apparently as a result of each thinking the other were from the Welsh club. Once police arrived, the two groups, totalling some 150 lads, realised what was happening and turned their attentions on them, hurling bricks and other missiles for almost half and hour. By the time police managed to calm things down, nine people had been arrested and a small number of policemen injured.

The end of April also saw a massive operation designed to deal with the increasing problem of hooliganism taking place on the railway network. The catalyst was an announcement by the British Transport police that the previous twelve months had seen a hundred per cent increase in the number of football-related arrests and, in a day of action involving some 500 officers attending eleven key games, the idea was to send a message that this kind of behaviour would no longer be tolerated.

Sadly, it backfired slightly with violent clashes between Sheffield United and Millwall fans taking place at Clapham Junction, while twenty Hull City and Sheffield Wednesday supporters were involved in a brawl at the city's main railway station. There was also major trouble at Nuneaton where a hundred fans fought with bottles and chairs at the town's train station ahead of the non-league clash between Borough and Kettering.

Thankfully, the game received a huge boost in May when Liverpool travelled to Istanbul and, in one of the greatest nights ever seen in European football, returned home with the Champions League trophy.

Inevitably, given the location of the final and the lingering legacy of Heysel, there had been concerns that trouble would once again feature in the post-match analysis and a huge operation had been put in place to prevent known trouble-makers from leaving the country. However, in the event those concerns proved unfounded and with no tournament to occupy the nation's football fans in the summer months, the entire country seemed to sit back and breath a collective sigh of relief. Sadly, any respite was to be short-lived, for yet again hooliganism soon returned to the public eye.

For some time, following incidents in various Northern towns, including Oldham, Stoke and Preston, organised hooligan groups had been increasingly linked with attacks on Muslim communities and, following the 7 July bombings in London, the rumours surrounding these links intensified. Key to this was the volume of discussion the bombings had generated on the internet, with various mobs being taunted as to their failure to deal with Muslim extremists who were seemingly roaming freely in their towns. This was especially true of L*t*n, home to the increasingly notorious Migs, who attracted all kinds of condemnation following the news that a number of the bombers had lived and worked in the town.

As the days progressed, newspapers began to run stories claiming that, as part of wider plans to generate a right-wing fuelled backlash, hooligan groups were being urged to set aside their rivalries and become involved in what was being called 'a greater cause'. In the event, these claims proved to be entirely unfounded. However, a planned friendly between Millwall and Iran at the New Den was called off for fear that the game would be targeted by right-wing protestors. Millwall's opening game against Leeds United at Elland Road also took on special significance when rumours began to circulate that groups from both clubs would use it to cause problems among the local community. However, these fears diminished when the South London club refused to take up their allocation of tickets.

July was further tainted by the arrival of the pre-season games, which saw the usual trouble at grounds up and down the country, including Hull, where nine people were arrested following clashes between home fans and Sunderland supporters, and Lincoln, where extra officers were needed to control trouble in the city centre involving local fans and visiting lads from Nottingham Forest.

These and similar incidents seemed to spark a rash of high-profile police activity with fans from all over England receiving long prison sentences for involvement in trouble at games the previous season. These included fourteen Leeds United fans who were sentenced to between four and twenty-one months for trouble at the game against Cardiff in January and five Villa fans who received between four and twelve months for trouble at Arsenal in March. However, this was merely a precursor to the main event, for in August the police came out with all guns blazing.

First, they announced that in an effort to prevent trouble at the 2006 World Cup they were going to take a nationwide zero-tolerance approach to hooliganism over the coming season. Then they announced exactly how they were going to do it. Key was what they called their 'national blueprint'. This was drawn up by the Association of Chief Police Officers and the Crown Prosecution Service (CPS) to ensure consistency in the way that all forty-two police forces in England and Wales dealt with anyone charged with a football-related offence. Also included was a range of new measures which included a much tougher approach to less serious offences, such as smashing windows and even swearing, together with measures designed to deal with anyone suspected of organising clashes either by phone or the internet.

Combined with the legislation already in place, the police now had at their disposal some of the most draconian anti-hooligan laws to be found anywhere. In fact, so stringent were they that magistrates had (and have) the power to apply a banning order to an individual if they play up while watching a game on a pub TV!

Finally, someone other than me began to voice concerns at the way things were going when the Football Supporters' Federation (FSF) came out with a statement suggesting that some genuine fans might be unfairly punished. In response, a spokesperson for the CPS was quoted as saying, 'We are not talking about people celebrating and having a beer, we are talking about people who do that and then smash the bar up.'

From that point on, the pressure on the hooligan scene was relentless, with forces up and down the country working with clubs to warn lads that if they stepped out of line, they would get hammered. Equally, intelligence prevented all kinds of pre-arranged meeting between rival mobs, most notably at Leicester in August, where two coach lads of L*t*n supporters were intercepted on their way to a meeting with the Baby Squad.

To an extent, this suppression worked. Certainly instances of large-scale disorder tailed off dramatically, but in some ways this simply played into the hands of those involved, because not only did it provide many of them with an excuse to take a step back for a while in the hope that they would be able to travel to Germany the following summer, but the failure to address the continued existence of the hooligan culture – always the fundamental flaw in the establishment's battle to defeat the hooligans – actually fuelled a degree of interest in the scene.

The fact that this was going on was a constant source of concern to the authorities, who were only too well aware that sooner or later things would explode. It finally happened in October, when fifty people were arrested after trouble flared in Newcastle following Sunderland's 3–2 defeat. At its height, over 300 were involved, including what Northumbria Police claimed were a number of 'well-known' football hooligans.

Ironically, the annual arrest figures released just days later showed an eleven per cent drop in the number of arrests at games the previous season and, once again, the police went into PR overdrive, claiming that the record levels of banning orders proved that they were winning the battle and reinforcing the message that the offensive would continue. The police even welcomed the controversial decision to invite ticket-less fans to visit Germany the following summer.

This optimism was further enhanced when England travelled to Geneva for a friendly against Argentina. This fixture would normally have caused concern, but on this occasion it was totally trouble-free.

The good news appeared to continue domestically, when even the Sheffield derby, a game traditionally tainted by violence, was devoid of any trouble between fans. This seemed to be a strong indication that the vociferous anti-hooligan campaigns were finally starting to pay dividends, but behind this façade a very different picture was emerging, because the police were increasingly being forced to employ ever larger anti-hooligan operations to deal with potential problems. For example, the Sheffield derby might well have been trouble-free, but it had required the biggest operation staged by South Yorkshire police in over three years to keep it like that. Indeed, all police leave was cancelled and prison cells across the region were emptied in anticipation of violence.

In part, this was driven by the understandable desire to maintain public confidence, as well as the need to apply as many banning orders as possible in an effort to prevent trouble at the forthcoming World Cup, but there can be little doubt that the authorities have become increasingly concerned that, in spite of the hard-line legislation, the threat of domestic hooliganism shows no sign of abating.

And they have good reason to be concerned. Sending uniformed officers and specially trained prosecutors to gather evidence on any England fans who cause trouble might look good to Joe Public, but most people with a degree of common sense know that these are merely PR gestures. It won't make any difference to what happens at home, either in the short or long term, and even in Germany the impact will almost certainly be negligible, because as we've seen on numerous occasions in the past, the major factor that will decide what happens at the World Cup is the local police. If they treat the England fans right and keep the local hools, the Poles, the Croatians and anyone else who fancies having a go well away, then things will be fine.

If they don't, then once again things will rapidly become ugly, for no other group of supporters in European football has the capacity to turn as quickly as those who watch the game in England, and if anyone is in any doubt about that, consider this. As I write, the papers are still discussing last weekend's game between Wolves and Cardiff City, which was held up when Welsh fans fought with police during half-time. This incident was apparently sparked by nothing more than a refusal to sell beer during the break, so goodness only knows what will happen should the German police decide to go wading into a group of lads and try to nick one of them for singing the 'Dambusters' theme. Sadly, I suspect time is going to tell.

PART TWO
MARCHING ON TOGETHER

CHAPTER THREE
THE HOOLIGANS

As someone who spends their life either writing, talking or researching the subject of football hooliganism, it should not come as any surprise to discover that I occasionally get astonishingly bored with it as a subject. The primary reason for that is not because I'm continually going over old ground or dealing with people I really don't want to deal with, but because I spend increasing periods of time reading, watching or listening to things that are presented by their authors as being wholly factual, but which are clearly almost entirely bullshit.

The most recent example to arrive on my desk was an article that appeared in one of the broadsheets claiming to have uncovered evidence that skinhead groups from Serbia, Croatia and the Czech Republic had formed a neo-Nazi hooligan alliance with the sole aim of causing mayhem at the World Cup finals in Germany. This story has about as much basis in fact as 'World War Two bomber found on moon', as anyone who knows anything about the history of the Balkan states would immediately understand.

Sadly, increasing numbers of journalists seem content to put their names to such obvious tripe, be it in print or on television, and that will continue until such time as those who pull these stunts are called to account by their peers, something I cannot see happening in the foreseeable future.

Much the same accusation can and should be levelled at those who inhabit the world of academia. The number of books and articles I've read that claim to be painstakingly researched studies of football-related violence, but which are obviously based on nothing more than the blindingly obvious, rumour, presumption, other people's work or even simple fabrication is staggering.

This isn't unique to hooliganism, of course. Both the media and academia are legendary for their ability to present myth and speculation as cast-iron fact, no matter what the subject, but the thing about hooliganism is that when something obviously wrong is written by Doctor This or Professor That or appears in one of the most respected newspapers in the world – or even one of the tackiest tabloids – people take it as the truth. That in itself is worrying enough, but if those people are in positions of power and are involved with forming any kind of football-related policy, it is extremely dangerous.

In part, this provides a perfect explanation as to why we are in the state we're in. Back in the early seventies, when the problem of crowd violence began to exert a major influence over the game, the sociologists, anthropologists and criminologists soon began to throw out their particular theories as to why lads were behaving as they did.

Instinctively they focussed on class, education, background and politics before rebellion, alienation and even anarchy were added to the list, until eventually they had all hooligans tagged as being working-class, right-wing, poorly educated products of broken homes, searching for some kind of family or sense of belonging. And because of where they came from, those theories were accepted by those in authority without question and, as a result, formed the basis on which all anti-hooligan thinking and policy was founded from that point on.

The problem was, of course, that they were only partially right in some respects, wholly wrong in others, plus they'd completely missed one of the most important aspects of the whole debate altogether, for while it was true that the majority of people involved in hooliganism were working class, that was simply because football was the working-class game. Similarly, from early on, the extreme right wing had recruited heavily from the terraces and, with the majority of academics holding left-wing or liberal views, the growth of hooliganism provided an obvious way to give credence to the perception of extreme right-wing politics being linked with violence and anger, while supporting the notion that the left was the peaceful and correct way forward.

Furthermore, many lads active at the time were reasonably educated and in decent, stable employment, with the majority, certainly in my experience, from traditional family backgrounds. But more importantly, while being a part of something as huge and anti-social as hooliganism was an attraction, few if any of those involved were searching for anything other than a good time – and that was exactly what hooliganism was providing them with week in and week out.

In reality, this 'good time' element has always been at the core of the entire issue. In that respect it's no different today than it was in the seventies or eighties, but in their need to apply rational reasoning to an irrational problem, it was the one thing that the theorists failed to recognise. The result was that the starting point they provided for the policy-makers was wrong, so the drive to deal with the problem has had a negligible effect. Indeed, other than handing the police ever more draconian legislation, it is debatable that there has been any real impact at all, a point surely proven by the fact that the culture of hooliganism has become so entrenched in the game that authority has all but given up trying to cure it, but instead seeks ever more complex ways to suppress it.

Astonishingly, despite this obvious failure, those theories still dictate thinking in certain circles. Only recently I got into a heated discussion with an MP who refused point-blank to accept that anyone involved in hooliganism could come from anything other than a dysfunctional background. How can you ever hope to move forward when you have people making decisions who are so blinkered to the realities of a situation?

The answer, quite simply, is that you can't, because one of the main reasons why the authorities will always be playing catch-up to the Saturday scene is because of the diversity of those involved in it – the exact opposite, in fact, of what the academic world would have everyone believe. Indeed, in this respect I believe that at this moment in time hooliganism is probably more complex in terms of the makeup of the participants than it has ever been. This not only makes it ever more difficult to police, but also makes it a whole lot more interesting to observe, not least because it proves that the evolutionary process is what drives the whole thing along. It has to. After all, if that wasn't the case it would have died out or been killed off years ago.

So just why does the hooligan problem persist? It is, after all, the most bizarre phenomenon which, when viewed objectively and in the cold light of day, is utterly ridiculous. Sadly, there is no single answer to that question, but there are instead numerous contributory factors which, when examined collectively, provide some kind of rudimentary reasoning. However, the starting point has to be an understanding of what hooliganism actually is, because, by its very nature, it means different things to different people.

In the early days of terrace battles, football specials and mobs of a hundred or more lads wrecking high streets and terrorising Joe Public just for the fun of it, defining it was relatively easy, because in the eyes of the majority, football was hooliganism and vice versa. These days, however, things are much more complicated, because as football has gradually moved itself out of the shadow of the kind of violence we routinely saw inside our grounds up until the mid- to late eighties, so the problem has faded or at least been pushed into the background. Given that, people's ideas of what hooliganism is will inevitably be based on personal experience and the fact that trouble is less evident these days means that the definition developed by a relative newcomer to the game will inevitably encompass a broader range of anti-social activities than one held by someone who has followed football for decades.

While this is understandable, an inevitable consequence is that behaviour once thought of as being traditionally associated with the terraces, such as chanting, standing up or even using foul language, is being increasingly criminalised, to the extent that some of these activities have now come to be regarded as acts of hooliganism among certain sections of the support. This would be fine were it not for the fact that both the authorities and increasing numbers of clubs are starting to empathise with this way of thinking and respond accordingly.

One of the most obvious examples of this is the way the game now deals with anyone who runs on the pitch – or rather 'invades' the playing surface (*sic*). This was a routine activity when I was a youth, but in these so called enlightened times a foray on to the grass will see you at best ejected and at worst banned for life from all football grounds, possibly with a criminal record firmly attached to your previously good name. In ninety-nine per cent of cases that isn't hooliganism, it's high spirits (or, more likely, too many spirits), but the clubs, the police and the courts treat anyone who does it as no less a hooligan than some Stone Island clad oik who travels across the country hellbent on kicking things off in a town centre pub. That is quite simply ridiculous.

The same thing applies to racist abuse. Yes, of course it has to be dealt with and to the full extent of the law, but it isn't anything to do with hooliganism at all. Indeed, many active football lads, particularly the black and Asian ones, find the very idea of racism abhorrent.

Unfortunately, the adoption of this wider definition has certain implications, because in terms of the bigger picture it is most definitely counterproductive. By applying the catch-all tag of 'hooligan' to anyone who is just being either stupid or a pain in the arse, you are actually diluting the impact of the terminology and therefore weakening the power of the word when describing the threat. More importantly, you actually make it easier for the active hard-core violent element to remain undetected by giving them more people to hide among. The result is that you unwittingly aid the perpetuation of the problem.

Of equal concern is that this ill-advised drive to sanitise football crowds is beginning to cause problems between specific groups of supporters, primarily because of the consequential and almost universally detrimental impact their presence is having on the atmosphere. Indeed, it is fair to say that many of those who have been fixtures and fittings at their grounds for years are growing ever more resentful of the new-breed prawn-sandwich brigade and the influence they are being allowed to wield over the game. This is never more evident than when the two collide, usually over the most trivial of incidents.

I have personally experienced this on two occasions and, as a result, am well aware of the anger and friction it can cause. The first involved someone who asked me to stop swearing because he was with his girlfriend and the second was when someone asked me to stop smoking because his wife was pregnant and it was bothering her. As you can imagine, given that I was sitting in the seat I'd sat in for years and had never seen a single one of the people complaining about me before, they were all given extremely short and colourful shrift, but the sad reality is that if either situation had turned ugly I could easily have ended up being ejected and possibly even banned.

A more disturbing example still came a few years ago when I was asked to provide expert testimony as a defence witness for two lads who had been arrested for using racist abuse at Highbury. Normally, I would steer clear of anything legal involving the issue of racism, but the fact that both were Arsenal fans and had been arrested for singing 'We hate Yids' at the North London derby was just too interesting to pass up, especially when I was told that the people who had lodged the complaint were a Jewish couple who claimed to have been Arsenal fans for years yet who swore on oath that in all their time following the Gunners they had never heard the term used in that context before.

Thankfully, I was able to provide ample proof that aside from having certain links with the Jewish faith, 'Yid' is also a term widely considered to be a reference to supporters of Tottenham Hotspur and, as a result, the judge accepted that there was no anti-Semitic intent and the lads both walked. However, had things gone differently, the fact that this was being regarded by the court as a football-related incident – and for that read hooliganism – meant that any subsequent sentence would have been extremely severe and those two men could easily have ended up in prison.

That is extremely worrying, not just for the individuals, but for the game as a whole, because there is a very real danger that by continuing to follow this 'catch-all' approach to hooliganism, football runs a strong risk of demonising large sections of its support and, as we saw in the eighties, that could prove to be extremely damaging, both in the short and long term.

It is therefore vital that the authorities move away from this way of thinking and embrace the notion that in its truest sense, 'proper' hooliganism has to involve a degree of either violence and/or aggression. Anything else is simply individuals being inconsiderate, selfish or unsociable. That's still unacceptable, of course, but nowhere near as serious a threat to the game as that provided by the continued presence of the violent element.

Ironically, to those involved, or at least the majority of them, no matter how it is defined hooliganism is always something done by someone else. I have met very few individuals over the years who would call themselves a 'hooligan', as most consider themselves to be nothing more than simple football lads. In part, this thinking originates from the almost universally held opinion that hooliganism is something you get into by choice and, as such, it's very much a victimless crime. After all, these days if you get into a row at all it's with a person who wants to get into a row with you and, since no one involved would ever complain to the police if they got a kicking, where's the problem?

Although slightly warped, there is a degree of logic in this way of thinking, although it is worth pointing out that these days the chances of even getting a slap at football, never mind a kicking, are remote. That isn't to say the threat or the intent aren't there, because they most certainly are, but thanks to wall-to-wall CCTV and oppressive policing, incidents of actual toe-to-toe violence of the kind we used to see routinely are becoming increasingly rare. So much so, in fact, that hostility towards rival fans is far more likely to manifest itself as aggressive posturing, language or gesturing than in any kind of physical contact.

However, far from detracting from hooliganism as an activity, this is actually one of the key reasons why it not only continues unchecked, but is actually growing, for in many respects this is the next logical step on the evolutionary road that hooliganism has always walked.

Think about it. The seventies and eighties were incredible times for those of us who followed football as a group of lads. Just about every game or journey had the potential for trouble and rarely a month went by without a major incident of some kind or another appearing in the national press. On top of that, the arrival and growth of the Casual culture provided just about everyone involved, including those of us on the edges, with the opportunity to expand our Saturday experience into new and fresh areas. Suddenly, we had what amounted to a uniform and the scene became as much about trainers, labels, music and even haircuts as it was about violence and playing up. By the early eighties Casual and hooliganism were pretty much one and the same, but if anything that made the scene even more attractive, as even the non-fighters were able to play their part by wearing the gear and simply looking the bollocks. Anyone who remembers the buzz of stepping off a football special in a strange town with a load of lads, each and every one of them geared up to fuck, will know that exciting doesn't even come close to describing what it felt like.

Yet in spite of the fact that the Casual scene was directly responsible for at least three murders in the early eighties and English hooligans had finally begun to cause mayhem whenever they travelled to Europe, neither the game nor the authorities seemed to be able to do anything about the increasingly organised and violent hooligan firms. Indeed, the majority of these had already come to think of themselves as all but untouchable. That was finally to change in 1985, the year the game finally cried 'enough'.

The catalyst for the clampdown was the infamous riot by Millwall fans at L*t*n. Although just one of a series of major incidents that had taken place that season, including Millwall's notorious attack on Bristol City, possibly the most well-planned football ambush of all time, the unique thing about events at Kenilworth Road was the presence of television cameras, which meant that footage of the trouble was broadcast around the world. The fact that it immediately spelt the end of the FA's bid to host Euro 88 sent the then prime minister Margaret Thatcher into apoplexy and she demanded the game clean up its act or she would do it for them.

However, even before that could happen, the English game was to be hit by two major tragedies, both of which were directly linked to hooliganism. First, a young football fan died and ninety-six policemen were injured when Leeds United fans rioted at Birmingham City and then, just eighteen days later, thirty-nine Italian football fans died at Heysel, when Liverpool supporters charged at them causing a wall to collapse.

However, anyone who thought the game had hit rock bottom was wrong. If anything, things seemed to get even worse when the now famous *Panorama* documentary 'Hooligan' took the organised hooligan groups, and in particular West Ham's Inter City Firm, into the homes of the nation. Suddenly, those involved took on a whole new aura of infamy, but even as this was happening the police were finally starting to get their act together. It didn't go entirely to plan initially, as various undercover operations fell apart, but gradually they began to get a grip on things. Slowly but surely the game moved away from the bear-pit mentality of old and, as it did so, the nature of hooliganism gradually began to shift towards a more underground and insular activity, which meant its grip on the game began to weaken.

By the time the game entered the post-Hillsborough era, not only had violence inside grounds become almost unheard of, but as a result of the pressure being exerted on the mobs by the police, even trouble outside was also becoming increasingly rare – something that continues to this day. Yet while the number of violent incidents has fallen dramatically since those days, the threat remains pretty much undiminished and that is almost entirely due to the fact that the scene remains just as attractive to potential participants as it ever was. One could even argue that it's even better, because the chances of having to spend a few days recovering from a battering or explain away a black eye (or a day in court) are severely diminished.

In many ways, this explains why we actually appear to be witnessing something of a growth in interest in the culture. After all, contrary to popular belief, no one really likes having the shit kicked out of them, but the really interesting thing is that this growth has come about in a number of ways and from a variety of sources. It is also yet another example of how complex this whole issue is.

The first and most obvious source is not newcomers, but returnees. Anyone who follows a particular club will be aware that in recent years there have been increasing numbers of older lads drifting back on to the scene. Faces who previously only ever turned out for the big occasions are now regular fixtures in pre-match pubs the length and breadth of the country.

While this has been attributed to everything from the demise of acid house to the seemingly obligatory mid-life crisis, the bottom line is that most have come back to try and recapture the buzz they used to get from being among a group of like-minded males and occasionally playing up a bit. Whether they rediscover that by following England, attending a particular game or even reading one of the numerous nostalgia-based hoolie lit tomes matters not. The fact is that they are returning in droves.

In some ways, this is a fantastic thing, for the returnees bring with them the kind of passion and humour that only those who have spent years travelling the country in dodgy transit vans and on moody trains can bring. However, it should also be remembered that while these days most might shy away from actively seeking out any kind of confrontation, preferring instead to laugh and joke their way through their Saturdays, no one should ever forget that, collectively, they know the score. No matter what situation they find, or indeed put, themselves in, it is almost certain that some if not all will have been through much worse at some point in the past. As a consequence, they will understand exactly how to react and when – something many a youth, or young copper come to that, has learnt to their cost.

This is best witnessed among those lads who travel away, for it is here, when freed from the shackles of the family and post-*Fever Pitch* elements of their own club's support that the real spirit of fandom can be seen. That's when it becomes more than a couple of hours on a Saturday afternoon and turns into a more involving experience. Trekking around the country week in and week out takes effort, but it pays huge dividends. The noise, the passion and the laughs are things you simply cannot get anywhere else.

When those same older lads travel abroad with the national side things get even better and, potentially, more dangerous. Many are veterans of the days when England on the road invariably meant major trouble and they know only too well how things work abroad. Armed with that knowledge and experience they certainly know how to piss people off should the mood take them, but, just as importantly, they know when to stop, unlike the younger lads who invariably continue to press buttons until things explode in their faces.

The youth, of course, are the other group who have seen an increase in their numbers in recent years, although for very different reasons. In many ways, this is one of the most interesting elements of this whole debate. A few years ago, when it released its annual arrest figures, NCIS issued a warning that more and more teenagers were becoming involved with organised firms. Like many, I ridiculed that as being yet another PR stunt to try and generate more funding, primarily because, as everyone knows, the 'under five' scene has been around for decades. Besides, just about every single lad I've ever met was at it way before they hit twenty, which does seem to prove that this is nothing new.

However, while nothing has happened since the release of that statement to make me change my opinion, it did make me start to look at the youth element and consider more deeply why they become involved with football at all. To be honest, it was a fascinating exercise for all kinds of reasons, not least because, as the father of a teenage lad, it made me realise how easily he could get sucked into the modern scene.

It has to be remembered, however, that there is a subtle difference between what we had then and what they have now. When I started going to watch games back in the early seventies the level of hooliganism was way beyond anything we have these days, but there was still a certain innocence about those of us who hung around the edges, threw the odd fool in the general direction of someone or did the odd bit of scouting. We knew what we were doing was wrong obviously, but we also knew that we wouldn't get into that much trouble if we got caught. What's more, we knew that if we didn't get lifted on the day, we weren't going to get lifted at all. Indeed, it's fair to say that for the most part the mere sight of a copper was usually enough of an incentive to behave – that and the fear of what our parents would do to us if we got caught.

Furthermore, those who wanted to move up the ladder and become a part of the main firm soon learnt how it all worked and what they would have to do to earn their place. Peer pressure was always a factor, of course, but if you didn't want to progress up the ranks, you simply stopped where you were or stopped altogether. It was the natural order of things and everyone understood it. These days, however, things are very different.

For a good number, it seems that the reasons they're involved are exactly the same as they were when we started. It's all about escaping the home and doing something by and for yourself, almost certainly for the first time. Factor in the idea of travelling around the country with lads who, through shared experiences, become mates for life, plus the simple truth that it sometimes involves doing things your mum would go apeshit about if she ever found out, and the attraction is magnified even further. What fourteen-year-old wouldn't want that?

To make matters even better, the explosion of hoolie lit in recent years means that the mystery which always surrounded the scene has dissipated. As a result, stuff we had to learn as teenagers during Tuesday night trips to places like Bolton and Cardiff can now be picked up without the hassle of even leaving your house.

Even the clothes side of things is easier. Where we had to go searching for labels such as Fila, Diadora, Lacoste and Tacchini to steal, these days you can pick them up anywhere and even the most sought-after labels are available relatively cheaply through online catalogues. If you're not that fussy, you can even find fakes at your local market for next to nothing. This was unthinkable when I was a kid, if only because it seems to be the exact opposite of what Casual is all about, but these days no one seems to give a toss if your gear is moody or not.

Most importantly of all, what makes the modern day scene so exciting to many young lads is that it has become more verbal than violent. And when you have a youth element who have been brought up with the notion that just about anything bar physical contact is acceptable behaviour these days, hooliganism provides the perfect environment for a bit of escapism. Providing, as it does, that sense of one-upmanship, personal empowerment and danger which have always been key attractions of the hooligan scene. I once labelled hooliganism 'the original dangerous sport' and nothing I have seen or heard has changed my mind. Indeed, if anything, time has reinforced that thinking. Let's face it, as a part-time activity it provides just about everything any young lad could possibly want, but that doesn't apply to all youths, for there are some who get involved for other, more personal reasons.

At this point, I may well have to eat a tiny bit of humble pie, because at the beginning of this chapter I had one of my all-too-frequent pops at the world of academia and the impact some of its 'theories' have had on the continued existence of hooliganism, most notably the idea that originated in the early eighties that we were all looking for some kind of affirmation or belonging when really all we wanted was a bloody good time. However, over the last couple of years I have begun to change my way of thinking on this and I am increasingly convinced that, in respect of certain individuals, this idea may have some degree of merit.

What started me off on this was a conversation I had with a group of lads at Watford. They were all well under eighteen, travelled home and away and were smartly dressed in that part-chav, part-Casual way. All of them had read just about everything they could possibly read on the scene and the thought of *The Football Factory* and *Green Street* hitting the screens had them positively salivating. It was almost like looking at myself thirty years ago. There was, however, one particular thing about them which struck me, which was that the majority were from single-parent families.

No shame in that, of course, but the more I reflected on it, the more it interested me and so I began to do a bit of digging around, not just at my own club, but at others. As I did so, I began to suspect that the demise of the traditional family has had a quite profound impact on football and the hooligan scene, for while the terraces have long provided the perfect environment for males to indulge in the kind of same-sex bonding which is vital to our gender's limited emotional growth, the sense of second family which derives from that camaraderie also has the potential to provide something else. And while it might not have been relevant to either me or the lads I knew when I was in my teens, it is clearly vital to many of the youngsters I've spoken to in recent years, because few of them had previously experienced it and some were perhaps unaware of how important it was until they came to walk through a turnstile. I am talking about a compelling and powerful male influence.

It is undoubtedly a sad reflection on modern day Britain that there are so many teenage lads who have little or no father figure at home, and it is even sadder still to think that for some the only opportunity they have to mix socially with older males comes via the Saturday scene. However, for many youngsters, that is the reality. The worry is that this influence will almost certainly be a negative one.

Thankfully, there will be plenty for whom a sense of right and wrong will be strong enough to restrict any anti-social behaviour to little more than a swagger and a bit of cockiness, but there are others for whom that will clearly not apply. For them, involvement with a group of lads not only provides a much needed sense of belonging, but also, in many respects, a sense of purpose. And among their number are plenty who crave the kind of respect that peer recognition provides. These lads, in particular, are a real danger, for they seem to have little or no intention of waiting for their acceptance into the ranks, but, instead, readily put themselves into situations where they are all but demanding attention. When you consider that many have little or no respect for law and order anyway, then you can see why, at certain clubs, we have youths with an almost feral sense of passion for the firm they aspire to be a central part of. After all, it provides them with things that they cannot get elsewhere and which rapidly become incredibly important to them as individuals.

Furthermore, the fact that the entire scene is governed by a set of unwritten rules and boundaries lends the whole thing a kind of 'honour-among-thieves' legitimacy, which allows them to justify to themselves why they behave in the way that they do. It also explains why increasing numbers not only consider a banning or tagging order as a badge of honour, but actually regard prison as an occupational hazard.

The irony, though, is that when you speak to some of these lads they genuinely believe that they are doing nothing seriously wrong. To them, the scene is simply a game played out between them, other lads and the police. This notion stems from the 'victimless crime' mentality previously mentioned and is reinforced by the fact that among football fans, and to a certain extent football itself, hooligan-ism has never really been criminalised. Indeed, despite all the negative publicity over the years, there is still no social stigma attached to it because the people involved are largely anonymous to those outside their immediate circle – something which, if anything, adds to the attraction.

Quite how the game will ever deal with this in the current climate escapes me. My personal opinion is that it will get worse before it gets better, because with more and more celebrity 'lads' (*sic*) wearing the gear and claiming links with this club or that club, and with the scene being portrayed in an almost favourable light in various books and films, the fact that someone might have a reputation for being the 'real deal' among their impressionable peers provides an even greater boost to their self-esteem. And as my own teenage lad frequently reminds me, to his generation it's all about respect.

However, young or old, there is another reason why we have witnessed an upsurge in numbers and interest over the last few years and that is the internet, possibly the most powerful tool ever handed to society. The beauty of the web is that it can deliver just about anything you want. Leaving aside the practical work and business aspects, if an individual wants to learn, inform, wind up, slag off, romance or even simply pass the time, it's the perfect medium. Just as importantly, it's everywhere – at home, in the office, on railways stations, in airports, in London, in China, on your laptop and even on your mobile phone. If you need it, you can get it easily and cheaply.

It's also all happened so fast. In terms of technology, the last decade has been breathtaking. In 2004, when my son-in-law was serving with the Royal Air Force in Iraq, my heavily pregnant daughter was able to see and talk to him every single night through her home PC. How incredible is that? Of course, initial fears that the web would be used to spread all kinds of death, destruction and debauchery have proved to be fairly well founded, but again, technology has provided the means with which to filter out all that crap, should you so wish, and in the main the web is a perfectly safe place for even young kids to surf around.

Yet incredibly, whether it's because they believe that the average football lad is too dumb to use a computer or too poor to actually have access to one, I regularly come across people who express surprise that hooliganism actually features on the web. Indeed, we still see the odd story in the press sensationalising the notion that apparently secret websites are regularly used to organise and plan violence.

Not surprisingly, the reality is somewhat different. For while in recent years the web has become an integral element of the scene for all kinds of reasons, just about every keyboard warrior knows that the vast majority of, if not all, the major football violence-related websites and message boards are monitored by either the police or the press, so trying to set anything up is pointless and potentially dangerous.

Things were different in the beginning, however, because fairly soon after the web began to become easily accessible to all and sundry, football began to feature prominently, and not long after that sites relating to the darker side of the game began to appear. To my mind the first person to really start the ball rolling was Paul Dodd, the former member of Carlisle United's Border City Firm, whose book *England's Number One* was one of the first hoolie biographies to hit Britain's book shelves. The message board on Paul's website rapidly became the forum for discussing anything to do with football violence and often that involved not only setting things up, but passing on details of incidents that had happened days or even hours previously to an increasingly eager and growing audience. It didn't even matter that most of it was complete bollocks. What was important was that it expanded the scene from Saturdays to every day and from grounds, streets and railway stations into front rooms and bedrooms.

As you would expect, the police had become aware of what was going on at a very early stage and expressed concern at the 'growing sophistication' of the hooligan scene, but what really got things going was when the media latched on to things. The catalyst for that came in the summer of 1999 when, in the aftermath of a major incident involving Cardiff and Millwall, the tabloids reported that the whole thing had been planned on the web and, in particular, on Paul Dodd's site.

As a marketing exercise, this was an incredible success, because not only did it garner a huge amount of publicity for Dodd's book, but it also afforded him a degree of notoriety which continues to this day. One newspaper even tagged him Britain's 'most notorious hooligan'. Having catapulted terms such as 'cyber hooligan' into the public psyche overnight, the tabloids continued their crusade and claimed a huge success when they eventually managed to have Dodd's site shut down. However, within days it was back and bigger than ever, thanks to the fact that just about everyone was looking for it.

Inevitably, the media obsession with Paul Dodd and his website backfired badly, because it kick-started what was, in effect, a hoolie dotcom boom. Within weeks, sites were springing up all over the place, until just about every single firm had its own website, while message boards dealing with every aspect of the scene, from England Youth to the non-league, rapidly appeared. Even European hooligans started to get in on the act with some quite amazing sites dedicated to providing highly detailed accounts of incidents in their home countries and even showing pictures of their lads in action.

It was all quite fun actually, but for those in the know, and particularly those who were still very much active, the continuing interest being shown by both the media and the police rendered the web effectively redundant as a planning tool. After all, what was the point of setting something up only to find the police sitting there waiting for you when you arrived?

There was, however, another problem, because the fact that the web was largely anonymous meant that all kinds of half-witted morons would pitch up on message boards and spout puerile and childish drivel. As a result, even some of the established boards rapidly descended into tedium, with childish exchanges about everything from sexual preferences to favourite crisps.

Thankfully, as time has passed the web has served football's least favourite culture reasonably well. There are plenty of sites where lads who know the score can exchange banter and information about recent – and not so recent – events, as well as let off steam about everything from politics to television. There are also those where abuse and wind-ups are the standard fare and others dealing with the retro side of things. From clothes and music right through to rose-tinted memories of terrace battles dating back to the seventies and eighties, it can all be found if you know where to look, and this is really what the web does best.

It provides a place where like-minded individuals can talk freely and openly about things which interest or fascinate them. And while some might accuse these hoolie sites of sanitising what was, and is, a very violent culture, the fact remains that for those who were there through what was in effect the 'golden age' of hooliganism, it was a life-shaping time, so why shouldn't they remember that with a degree of fondness?

I know this is going to seem odd given just about everything I have said or written in recent years, but rightly or wrongly, I know I do. What the game has to do is to ensure that those who are at it today aren't sitting here thinking the same things in twenty years' time. That really would be a tragedy for all of us.

CHAPTER FOUR
THE MEDIA

In my previous book Barmy Army I wrote a long and detailed attack on the media and its role within the continued existence of hooliganism. That argument contained the following paragraph:

> There is a point to be made here and it is founded on one of the most unpalatable truths I have ever been forced to write; that the British press love football hooliganism. I do not make that statement lightly, but it is one that is hard to argue against. Hooliganism provides everything a good story should have; drama, tension, fear and villains. Throw in a bit of shame and occasionally the odd pinch of xenophobia and you have perfect press. In a responsible climate, such press would be full of condemnation and demanding action from the authorities. Yet in this instance, although we have had plenty of condemnation over the years, we have seen little in the way of action. The reason for that is that the majority of journalists are driven not by the desire to expose the truth, but the need to shift papers and draw viewers. And when you have something like football violence, which explodes on to the scene every so often and makes great copy, why on earth would you want to try and stop it?

Not surprisingly, the reaction from within the journalistic community ranged from outrage to grudging agreement, while the response from football fans was universal applause. But I stood, and sadly remain standing, behind that paragraph, because, shamefully, even though I wrote it over five years ago, every single word is as relevant today as it was back then.

Proof, if any were needed, that the pursuit of headlines and viewers is all too often more important than the truth isn't hard to find. A brief search through my own files reveals numerous accusations about journalists 'constructing' stories on racist fans for a tabloid newspaper and television news crews paying lads to stage fights or burn flags abroad. The latter is a particularly favoured and well-known tactic, although whenever the news crews are questioned about it, of course they say it never, ever happens.

Furthermore, we have seen news organisations portray obviously foreign football hooligans as English to lend credence to an otherwise flimsy story and listened to so-called experts make statements on news programmes that are so blindingly false it beggars belief. Equally, we have seen lads who have travelled abroad to follow either club or country being portrayed as the scum of the earth, simply for having the audacity to try and protect themselves when being attacked by local fans or police. One only has to think back to the murders of Chris Loftus and Kevin Speight in Istanbul to see the truth in that.

The fact that those horrific scenes were repeatedly broadcast on national television that night was shameful enough, but when you consider that the Leeds fans were initially portrayed as the aggressors, it's simply beyond belief. Indeed, it was only when the full horror of that night began to filter through that the news groups finally realised what had gone on and changed the tone of the reporting, but it was late, way too late.

However, if ever there was an incident that highlighted to me just how irresponsible certain sections of the media can be, it happened prior to England's trip to Turkey in 2003. This match was a potential flash point and the FA had already refused its ticket allocation in an effort to avoid any attempt by English hooligans to extract revenge for those two murders, when, out of the blue, a story appeared in one of the tabloids about videos of hooliganism being sold over the web. Some of the film was CCTV footage obtained from a variety of sources, while other film came from documentaries and even the odd hand-held mini-cam. As it happened, I knew one of the guys who was selling it and had even corresponded with him on many occasions, largely because I actually thought he'd had a good idea, yet to the tabloid press, some of whom seemed to have no problem filling pages with adverts for porn, the fact that people were making money out of this violence was nothing less than an outrage. And in the usual pre-tournament, anti-hooligan frenzy, the story remained in the public eye for a good few days, with accusations even being levelled that this was all part of some plot to stoke up trouble ahead of the tournament and then exploit it for financial gain.

Thankfully, the interest in this total non-story eventually died down, but a few weeks later I was contacted by a guy from one of the major television news networks who was looking to do an exposé on one of the people who was selling these videos. Ironically, it was the very same guy I had been corresponding with. When I pointed out to the journalist concerned that the very worst thing this guy might possibly have been guilty of was the odd copyright infringement, his enthusiasm remained undimmed, so out of curiosity I agreed to get together with him a few days later to find out what he wanted.

When we met, I immediately began to suspect that something was very wrong, a feeling heightened when he asked that we go outside, because it was quieter, and made even worse when he played me a recording of a telephone conversation he'd had with the guy concerned the day before. As talk progressed to the possibility of obtaining film of specific incidents and then somehow got round to right-wing politics, I actually began to wonder if he had a tape recorder or, worse, a camera whirring away even as we were talking.

It soon became clear, though, that I had no need to worry, because I was not his 'target'. That was the guy selling the videos and his plan was to meet him and record that meeting on a hidden camera for a news item about the selling of hooligan footage.

When I asked him what the point of this was, he told me that he had only recently been hired and was in fact still on probation. This had seemed to be the perfect story to establish his credentials as an undercover reporter who was prepared to take risks, the inference being that if he was selling film of violence, the guy must obviously be violent.

Stunned by this, I asked him what he wanted from me and the simple answer was advice. Although he had a cursory knowledge of hooliganism, he knew very little about the group to which this lad belonged and the last thing he wanted, for obvious reasons, was to be sussed. Thankfully, I had another meeting to go to and so, promising him that I would be in touch after I had thought about his request, I headed off. However, by that point every single thing I had ever thought about the media had been reinforced.

Here was a journalist prepared to destroy the reputation of a person who in reality was doing little or nothing wrong except trying to make a few quid on the side, simply to try to further his own career. As if that wasn't bad enough, he had clearly given no thought to the bigger picture, because the potential consequences of broadcasting something like this could have been immense. Inevitably, the story would have been billed as some kind of sensationalist revelation, which would simply have added to the concern about England fans ahead of the forthcoming tournament, yet in truth, it was a nothing story about nothing.

In the event, it never materialised anyway, largely because when I got home I contacted the guy selling the videos and warned him that someone was on his case, so for a while at least he kept a low profile. He was lucky, but over the years there have been plenty who have not been so fortunate and who have been left to deal with the consequences of similar examples of irresponsible journalism. Lads returning from trips overseas, for example, have been slaughtered in the past, simply for being foolish enough to speak to the press at airports and give their own, often horrific, experiences.

I am not for one moment suggesting that all journalists are rotten, far from it. There are plenty of decent sports reporters working in TV, radio and print who know the realities of life as a football fan, especially those fans who travel with either club or country. Similarly, I wouldn't dare to even intimate that there are not plenty of active lads who actually do deserve to be spread across the tabloids or the television screen. The problem is that far too often decisions are taken by people sitting behind desks or in edit suites who don't have that same experience, with the result that the public is fed perceptions of people or incidents that are at best misguided or at worst entirely wrong.

To me, this is nothing less than abuse of power, because, once in place, those perceptions are very difficult to rebuild, not least because those involved in putting the story together would have to admit to making a mistake and I know enough people in that industry to know that the chances of that happening are fairly remote!

The irony of this is that if we are ever to see any kind of solution to the issue of hooliganism, the media is the one group capable of securing it. This is especially true of the tabloids for, unlike the FA or the police, they have a direct and daily link to Joe Public. Even better, that link is forged on a very tentative kind of brand loyalty, something every newspaper owner and editor is fiercely aware of. Indeed, despite every effort to repair the damage, the *Sun* is still shunned in large parts of Liverpool after it printed a scurrilous headline the day after the 1989 Hillsborough disaster.

Of course, almost certainly for the reasons I outline above, the desire to search for a solution does not seem to be anywhere on the media agenda. Instead, it seems happy to sit back and wait for the next outbreak of football-related violence, when it will be able to indulge in the type of sensationalist over-exaggerating and moralising we have seen a thousand times before. And, once again, we will see the same tired old stereotypes reinforced and public opinion hardened against the decent law-abiding football fans who, let us never forget, form the vast majority of the followers of our national game.

This is not only a tragedy for the game and the people who follow it, but it is incredibly short-sighted. On numerous occasions in the past we have seen how the public can react badly to negative media campaigns relating to football. The best example of this was Euro 96, when both the *Mirror* and the *Sun* ran xenophobic headlines ahead of the game against Germany. In previous times 'Achtung Surrender' and 'Let's Blitz Fritz' would have gone down a storm, but what both papers had failed to realise was that by that point in the tournament the mood of the nation had changed completely. Not only had the threat of large-scale hooliganism, which itself had been whipped up by the media, proved to be ill-founded, but the nation as a whole had fallen back in love with the game and were relishing the fact that the game had come home. More importantly, England had fallen in love with itself. Even to the extent that the cross of St George, so long derided as a symbol of the extreme right wing, had been embraced by much of the population and was to be seen everywhere.

Not surprisingly, the press realised its error of judgement almost immediately and changed its approach, yet to this day there can be little doubt that whenever England travels, the desire for an outbreak of trouble remains as real as it ever was at editorial desks. We have seen it everywhere from Charleroi to Cardiff.

In truth, this desire is outdated, because the days of hooligan league tables and crazed headlines urging for the return of birching and National Service are, thankfully, long gone. Yes, of course there has been trouble involving English football fans both at home and on their travels, but in the main they are in the past. For example, the last major trouble inside a stadium in England was Watford versus L*t*n in September 2002 and even outside grounds serious incidents have been rare. Abroad, incidents are even less frequent and usually involve nothing more serious than a few lads getting drunk and being loud – a reflection on the state of our nation rather than on our national game.

Instead, as a result of numerous factors, ranging from the use of banning orders and aggressive policing right through to all-seater stadia and even simple boredom with the hooligan lifestyle, we have a new breed of travelling support, one that includes more women than ever before, even whole families, and which travels not with hate in its heart, but with hope, pride and above all a desire for fun.

The one thing we don't have is positive coverage of that support and to many people, myself included, that is something of a mystery. After all, it seems obvious to me that if the press were to adopt the same approach to England football fans as it does to the nation's cricket supporters, everyone would benefit, be it through an improved image for the game, the fans or even the nation. To be brutally honest, that would be more accurate anyway, for now that the days of the respective sports being reflections of the class system are (surely) consigned to history, the two groups are essentially exactly the same anyway, not simply in their approach to their 'role' as fans and ambassadors for their sport and their country, but also in their makeup. One only has to glance around the perimeter of any ground where the English cricket team is playing to see flags and banners bearing the names of football clubs from all over the UK, yet in spite of this one group is largely pilloried at every turn and the other trumpeted as the way forward. Why?

To me, the answer to that question is a simple one. Leaving aside the issue of headlines and graphic pictures, the one thing all media groups are afraid of is being made to look stupid and should the unthinkable happen and we have a flashback to the bad old days, be it in Germany or anywhere else, the paper that openly backed the fans would inevitably be made to backtrack. No newspaper likes to eat humble pie or, worse, be made to eat it.

The real tragedy, of course, is that despite the success of Japan, Portugal, Istanbul and everywhere else England or an English side has played in recent years, the baggage of history dictates that the fear of disorder will always haunt us on our travels. The English, never the most popular race across the Channel anyway, remain the target for hooligan groups throughout Europe and it galls me to say it, but that is unlikely to change for the foreseeable future.

Indeed, as the 2006 World Cup approaches I have already been contacted by a number of journalists asking me to help them infiltrate hooligan groups or work with them to help 'expose' the threat of racism among the travelling support. There is nothing new in that, it happens every time England heads for a tournament and every time these requests receive a curt no, not simply because I disagree vehemently with that kind of reporting, but because there are better stories to be had.

Of course, hooliganism and racism at football have to be reported, but it must be balanced and most certainly should not be sensationalised. However, in recent years scores of travelling supporters have had the courage to stick their heads above the parapet and do their bit to try and change the image of our game abroad, so is it really too much to expect that one of our media groups might one day have the bottle to follow suit and back them to the hilt? Not just in word, but in deed? Or is it still the case that as far as the media is concerned, the working-class image of sport dictates that there is room for only one English Barmy Army? A second would be just too much to contemplate, especially when it has historically provided such good press.

CHAPTER FIVE
HOOLIE LIT

If anything provides proof that hooliganism is alive and well it is the continued existence of, and fascination with, the literary genre that has become known as 'hoolie lit'.

To a certain extent, the people to blame for this are my brother and I. After all, while we certainly weren't the first to write about hooliganism, when we wrote *Everywhere We Go*, a full six years after Colin Ward's excellent book *Steaming In* had been published, the fact that it was easy to read and spoke in a language that people could understand not only struck a chord with the public and publishers alike, but highlighted the simple truth that writing for publication wasn't some mysterious activity undertaken by chain-smoking, alcoholic weirdoes or sad, self-obsessed loners, but was, largely thanks to word processors, relatively normal and above all easy. It was very much a case of 'if we could do it, anyone could!'

As a result, people like Cass Pennant, Martin Knight, Chris Brown and a host of others followed us into print with great success and a genre was born, the consequence being that book shelves the length and breadth of Britain (and beyond) now positively bulge with everything from academic studies (*sic*) to autobiographies and even parodies of the hooligan and Casual culture. And believe me, they sell, not in the same volumes as 'lad lit' and certainly nothing like 'chic lit', but enough to keep the various publishers happy and ensure that the flow will continue for some considerable time. Indeed, I know of at least two books due for publication shortly after the forthcoming World Cup, with many more in the planning stage.

For the authors and fans of hoolie lit this is good news, but there are plenty who are not so happy. The authorities are at the front of the queue of people who not only consider these books as being little more than irresponsible celebrations of a form of violence they are desperate to eradicate, but also regard certain titles as being no better than training guides for wannabe thugs. But if the authorities head the queue, not far behind is the media. As recently as August 2005, the *Daily Express* ran a full-page story under the banner headline 'Glut of books on soccer yobs is stoking up violence', which featured quotes from numerous politicians and ex-policemen condemning the existence of these books and accusing the people who read them as being 'impressionable' and 'easily manipulated'. Previous articles have attacked the publishers for cynical exploitation, while the various authors have all been condemned at one time or another. Andy Nicholls, who wrote *Scally*, was even banned from attending games at Goodison Park for daring to write about his exploits as one of Everton's firm.

Of course, when they can't attack the content of the book or the author, they go after the quality of the writing. Mundane, amateurish and even juvenile are all accusations thrown at hoolie lit over the years, often by magazines such as *When Saturday Comes*, whose contributors positively relish every opportunity to rubbish any tale from within the hoolie ranks with a seemingly constant barrage of holier-than-thou, anti-hooligan-author drivel. This is ironic, given that the primary quality needed by the average *When Saturday Comes* contributor seems to be the ability to seek out ever more obscure and pointless aspects of the great game to bleat about.

Not surprisingly, I have little sympathy with anyone who has a problem with these books, no matter what approach they take to the subject matter. Yes, there is little doubt that some of them are badly written and one could even argue that some of them aren't worthy of publication, but I know how tough it is to write a book and how much harder it is to find a publisher, and anyone who pulls it off deserves nothing but respect, especially when, unlike many more supposedly 'worthy' books that sell next to no copies and sit on library shelves untouched for years, hoolie lit actually has a market.

More importantly, the point most people seem to miss when they criticise these books is that they are, in the main, non-fiction. And while the accuracy of the content is occasionally questionable, the bottom line is that they all have a basis in fact. Like it or not, hooliganism and the culture of Casual that grew from within it are an important part of football's history and their existence undoubtedly shaped the great game forever, so why shouldn't that be documented by the very people who were involved in it?

As for being 'training guides', does that really need any comment from me? Yes, of course these books make people aware of certain things and most definitely explain the whos, whys and wherefores, but are people that foolish to believe that any of these nostalgia-fuelled contributions to the genre have ever actually enticed anyone into a life of hooliganism?

Ironically, where these accusations do hold some degree of accuracy is in the fictional representations of the culture. When I set out to write *Green Street*, a film about an American student, played by Elijah Wood, who comes to England and gets involved with a fictional hooligan firm at West Ham United, the idea that the release would kick-start a fledgling hooligan scene in the US was, and remains, a very real one. The prime reason for this is that, grunge aside, youth culture in the US seems mainly to revolve around hip-hop and there are increasing numbers of white teenagers who are becoming frustrated at the lack of something that they can claim for themselves. Hooliganism, or more specifically Casual, could easily fit that bill, with disastrous consequences for the game there.

Thankfully, so far that fear has yet to materialise, yet it does highlight the fact that fiction is potentially far more powerful than non-fiction. It is, after all, made up and as a result authors can let loose and create whatever scenarios and characters they like. For many people the fictional accounts of hooligan life are actually more readable than the real-life stuff, given that they are by definition, devoid of any claims, rumours or bullshit, yet strangely few have managed to make it into print. John King's excellent book *The Football Factory* enjoyed huge success and certainly took the genre, and the author, into the literary mainstream, while Kevin Sampson's *Awaydays* is held in very high regard. Even my own two attempts, *The Crew* and *Top Dog*, did well enough, yet aside from these four books there has been nothing of note in recent years. What makes this even more surprising is that the film rights to all four of those books were snapped up and, although so far only *The Football Factory* has made it to the screen, *The Crew* is certainly well on the way to following it.

Quite why this is is open to debate, but it is certainly not for the lack of a market or, indeed, literary talent. In the late nineties I began an internet writing circle with the aim of getting more lads into print and the quality of some of the fictional writing was simply breathtaking. One reason, possibly the main reason, is that fictional accounts have all tended to paint the hooligan lifestyle in a positive light and as a result have attracted accusations of glorification. And while most authors relish charges like that, if only for the PR they bring, they are a publisher's worst nightmare and something few seem willing to confront. This is possibly because hooliganism isn't like the Krays or even the SAS; it is real, ugly and, more importantly, anyone can experience it on any given Saturday. Equally, it continues to blight the great game, so why court controversy when you don't need to?

Much the same can be said of television. On the very few occasions hooliganism has been dramatised on the small screen, those involved are universally portrayed as being unhinged, right-wing morons who are inevitably involved in some kind of criminal activity. In the main, this is down to bad research and/or writing, but it is also fair to say that the use of a negative stereotype is always far easier to defend than something closer to reality. Perish the thought that hooligans would be normal guys with normal jobs!

The film industry, however, is not so fearful of controversy. Indeed, it actively courts it, but that's because it's about making money – no more, no less – and the unexpected success of the low-budget adaptation of *The Football Factory*, boosted by a quite brilliant publicity coup involving pirated copies of the film selling on just about every market in the land, certainly made many people within that industry sit up and take notice. So much so, in fact, that when news of the project first broke I received a flood of enquiries about the film rights for both *The Crew* and *Top Dog*, and I know other authors were similarly approached. Soul Crew even had Robert Carlyle and Irvine Welsh attached to the script.

As premiere time for *The Football Factory* approached and news broke that Elijah Wood would be making a hooligan movie in London, things got even crazier. Within weeks, there were even more films in the early stages of production, including a biography of Cass Pennant. Quite how many of those will actually make it to the big screen remains to be seen, but while it is very exciting for everyone involved, as well as for those of us who are keen to watch them, there can be little doubt that if the authorities have cause to be worried about anything, it is this – for one very simple reason.

It is one thing sitting down and taking a few days to read a book. It is quite another to sit down and spend two hours watching a film. When you can do that with your mates, in the comfort of your own home and maybe with a few beers, so much the better. You can even replay the good bits, over and over and over again. It's great fun if you're twenty or thirty or older and can compare it to the 'good old days' – or rip it apart for being inaccurate – but when you're fifteen, or maybe even younger, it takes on a whole new meaning, simply because you have nothing to compare it to. And when hooliganism looks as much fun as it is usually made to look on screen, can it really be that much of a surprise that so many teenagers are getting interested?

After all, those old arguments of 'belonging' and 'family' which applied to many of us when we were younger apply equally to the current generation, possibly even more so given that the social pressures on them come from all angles and the future for many is sadly so bleak. So why wouldn't being part of an anti-social, even anarchic 'gang' be appealing?

I am not for one moment suggesting that films are entirely to blame for the recent rise in the number of 'under five' groups linked to clubs, or the fact that most grounds on matchdays these days seem to be surrounded by teenage lads wearing the right gear and all too often acting up, but they certainly haven't helped. The problem for the authorities is that while people want to watch these films, the film industry will keep churning them out, and the really worrying thing is that there is absolutely nothing anyone can do about it except wait and hope the interest fades. And from where I sit, there is no hope of that happening for some considerable time yet.

Strangely, given their seemingly obsessive fixation with violence, one area that hasn't been able to capitalise on the interest in hooliganism has been the games industry. Indeed, as far as I know there has been only one effort – *Hooligans, Storm Over Europe.* Launched in a blaze of publicity, the game allowed the player to set up and lead their own hooligan gang as they battled their way across Europe. The idea was great, the graphics were fun and there was even a facility to play online with other gamers.

Surprisingly, given the nature of some of the other games on open sale, the concept had the authorities and the media incandescent with rage. So much so that within weeks of its release just about every store in the land was refusing to stock it, with the inevitable result that it achieved cult status very quickly. But there was one problem, playing it became extremely boring very quickly, something those who railed against it would have rapidly realised had they bothered to play it. Indeed, they could have saved everyone a great deal of grief by simply ignoring it and letting it fade away on its own.

However, I can say with some degree of certainty that the games industry has most certainly not given up on this subject yet. 'Beat-em-ups' form a huge part of its market and with hooliganism such a curious social phenomenon all it requires is the right plot or even the right tie-in and it will be away again. And with censorship all but non-existent in the games industry, let alone the bedrooms of pre-pubescent teenage boys, that's something we should all be worried about.

In recent years, hooliganism has been written about from all kinds of angles. Those who were once at it, those who are still at it, those who love it, those who hate it – they've almost all had their turn at one point or another. Yet there is one area that has thus far received little or no attention from within the world of hoolie lit and quite why this is so remains a mystery to me, because in many ways it is the most secretive and misunderstood element of this fascinating issue and it would certainly be more worthy – and certainly more controversial – than yet another 'we did this, they did that'-type exposé of the scene. I am, of course, talking about the people who have come to be widely regarded by those 'in the know' as British football's biggest and most organised mob. I am talking about the police.

What would make this so intriguing to me is not so much the operational aspect, but more the personal side. I have spoken to enough coppers over the years to know that many veterans of football have some quite amazing stories to tell. Indeed, some have featured in previous books. For example, a good number of the officers who were in the front line during the riot after the Millwall versus Birmingham play-off game in 2002 regard it as one of the most terrifying experiences of their careers, while the exploits of some of those football intelligence officers who have sailed a bit close to the wind with the lads they are supposed to be keeping an eye on would make for great reading.

Sadly, as yet there is no sign of such a book and I suspect one of the main reasons for that is because, unless it is in relation to specific high-profile cases, most policemen seem to be quite wary of committing anything to print for fear it will reflect badly on the force. Similarly, I can state from experience that the upper echelons of the police are far from accommodating when questioned on the hooligan issue, so I'm guessing they wouldn't be overly supportive of the idea either. In fact, I know they're not because I've asked them.

That is a great shame. Like many people who follow football I would like to read more about how hooliganism as a culture is perceived by those charged with the responsibility of dealing with it. After all, it is clearly a very difficult and occasionally extremely dangerous job. Furthermore, if we are ever to fully understand the nature of the hooligan menace then it is vital that the experiences of all those involved are taken into account. Obviously that must include those who uphold the law.

However, the fact that they are seemingly so reluctant to talk about their personal experiences illustrates perfectly one of the fundamental problems that has traditionally affected the relationship between football fans and the police and that is the existence of an 'us and them' situation. It is a sad fact that over the years many football fans have come to regard the representatives of law and order as something akin to an enemy. While that in itself is bad enough, the real tragedy is that this isn't simply limited to the Saturday lads. Oh no, it extends right across the board.

At this point I should make it clear that on a personal level I am no fan of the boys in blue and I have never made any secret of that. Oh for sure they're the first people I'd call on if my family needed protection or assistance and I feel nothing but admiration and respect for the men and women who routinely place themselves in the front line of the fight against terrorism and organised crime. In that sense, the British police are the finest in the world. No doubt. But when it comes to football, things are different – very different.

However, before we get into all that, in the absence of any contribution from the police, we need to briefly examine how the police have dealt with the problem of hooliganism in the past, for they are obviously central to the future of this most complex of issues, given that they have played such an important part in its history.

It is fairly well accepted that of all the nations where the great game is played, England has had by far and away the biggest problem with hooliganism. This is not something we should be proud of really, but it's hardly surprising given that we have more clubs and a higher percentage of travelling fans than any other country on earth.

The fact that this situation has existed for more than a few decades now is nothing less than a disgrace and, while I frequently blame all and sundry for that, I know as well as anyone that the real culprits are the Saturday lads themselves. If they hadn't driven the culture of violence onto the terraces of England back in the seventies and kept it rolling through the eighties and nineties, right up to the present day, then you would not be reading this book. It really is as simple as that.

But they did and one of the consequences has been that the police in this country have become universally regarded as the best anti-hooligan force there is. Again, it's not something we should be proud of, because it clearly illustrates an abject and long-term failure to bring the problem to any kind of a resolution. However, as I have stated on many occasions, I do not believe that the police should be responsible for that resolution, because that's the job of the game and the Government. The police's role is to uphold the law of the land and react to things on the ground, as and where necessary. To this end, over the years they have developed all kinds of methods and tactics to try and carry out this duty and contain the hooligans' activities. Many of these approaches have been aided by the development and use of increasingly sophisticated technology, while others involve good old basic policing.

In the seventies and eighties the most visible example of this was the use of escorts. At a time when the bulk of the travelling support at many clubs comprised of active lads, the police would simply surround them with bodies, dogs and even horses and literally drive them from the railway station or coach park to the ground. Then, afterwards, they would simply herd them right back and away.

It was incredibly confrontational, but for those of us who followed our clubs away, extremely exciting. Being marched through the streets like some kind of invading army, especially at somewhere like Stoke or Derby where the locals were often hostile, was a real buzz, especially when the police were busily winding everyone up or things kicked off as they frequently did. More often than not, this would involve some kind of ambush at a particular spot en route or local lads infiltrating the escort and giving it large. Something that took incredible nerve given that they often came unstuck.

Inside the grounds things were often equally exciting (or terrifying, depending on who you followed and where you were). In the days before clubs really got their act together, mobs would sometimes be separated by nothing more than a single line of policemen – with inevitable results. At a time when the taking of ends was the standard aim for all visiting mobs, it was certainly not uncommon for fights to spill over on to the playing surface.

By the end of the seventies just about every club in the land had erected fences around the pitch and pens to keep the fans apart, and the amount of trouble inside grounds began to decline. As a result, if things did kick off inside the pens the police, sure in the knowledge that the trouble would be contained in a relatively small area, would often let it continue for a while before going in to deal with those involved.

Or at least some police forces would, for one of the criticisms often levelled at the police back then was that their approach to hooliganism varied from force to force and even from matchday commander to matchday commander. It is certainly fair to say that some constabularies would allow lads to get away with things that would result in arrest in another part of the country.

Thankfully, those days have long-since been consigned to history, as has the use of escorts. These days, officers are posted at various points around the ground with the odd beat officer or van shadowing any suspicious group. Similarly, inside grounds the move toward police-free matches continues apace, with stewards increasingly employed to deal with security issues, albeit under the watchful eyes of the boys in blue. Not as much fun, but just as effective.

Another tactic the police began to employ early on was the use of plain clothes officers to gather information and infiltrate hooligan groups. This actually first began at the request of the FA back in the mid-sixties, when it was becoming increasingly concerned at the growing number of incidents involving travelling fans. By the eighties this had become one of the most important weapons in the fight against the hooligans, largely because the police had somehow convinced both themselves and the media that the organised groups were becoming so structured that sooner or later a move towards more recognised criminal activities was inevitable. Hence, in an effort to smash the organised firms once and for all, they handed numerous officers new identities and tasked them with 'living the life' to get as far inside the mobs as they possibly could. In 1986, a year after Heysel and the Millwall riot at L*t*n, they finally struck. And they did so in the full glare of the media spotlight.

One of the first to hear the '6 o'clock knock' was Chelsea. On 26 March 1986 Operation Own Goal (a title that was to prove strangely prophetic) saw seven men, alleged to be the ringleaders of the so-called Head-hunters, dragged from their beds and hauled into court. Over the next four years clubs, including Leeds United, West Ham, Millwall, Wolves, Manchester United and Birmingham City, were targeted in this way, with the majority of men arrested charged with conspiracy to commit affray or conspiracy to commit violence. For those who pleaded guilty, justice was swift and heavy, with sentences ranging from long periods of community service right through to ten years' imprisonment.

However, it quickly transpired that not all the convictions were safe. In some cases evidence, which ranged from possession of calling-cards to ownership of weapons, was allegedly tampered with or even falsified and the behaviour of the undercover officers was frequently called to account. As a consequence, within four years a number of operations, including Own Goal (Chelsea), Full-time (West Ham and Millwall), White Horse (West Ham), Back Yard (Crystal Palace) and Spoonbill (L*t*n), had collapsed with all charges dropped. Despite these very high-profile and very expensive failures, the use of infiltration as a source of intelligence-gathering continues to this day. However, with the organised groups becoming ever more cautious of both the police and the media, outsiders are increasingly regarded with suspicion.

Another intelligence-gathering technique universally employed in this country is the use of dedicated football intelligence officers (FIOs). First pioneered at Euro 88 and now widely copied across Europe, FIOs work closely with the clubs to which they are attached to identify local hooligans and pass on details of their movements during away trips. This has proven to be extremely effective over the years and has certainly worked well during international tournaments. However, as a weapon it has had a number of downsides. Not only does the sight of an FIO invariably raise the hackles of the Saturday lads, but over the years certain FIOs have forged relationships bordering on friendships with some of the people they are supposed to be keeping an eye on. It has even been alleged that in some instances they have actually passed on information to facilitate incidents or help their own lads avoid arrest. This was certainly widely reported during Euro 2000, when the Belgian police were busily running amok and attacking anybody English.

The other downside is that supporters are occasionally placed in situations where they look to their own FIO for help and when that isn't forthcoming problems inevitably ensue in the aftermath. The most high-profile example of this was in April 2000, when the two Leeds United fans were murdered by Galatasaray supporters in Istanbul. Many of the Leeds lads involved in that incident claim that shortly before the attack took place their FIO had told them he was perfectly happy with the situation and was going for a meal. This was totally at odds with the officer's version of events, for he claimed that he had witnessed the entire incident, but had been unable to intervene because he had not been in uniform. Not surprisingly, this disparity was the cause of much anger after the event, with many Leeds fans inevitably levelling a degree of blame in his direction.

In the main, however, most FIOs manage to strike exactly the right balance between the requirements of their role and the need to forge a working relationship with supporters who potentially could be a problem to them. As a deterrent, they can be mightily effective.

Of course, aside from standard policing the other weapon employed to combat the threat of violence is technology. Indeed, we have seen some quite astonishing developments in this area in recent years. The most high-profile of these has been in the use of CCTV. First used in the mid-seventies, CCTV has now become one of the most vital tools in the battle not just to police the hooligans inside grounds, but to track them in the streets outside and supply the evidence to convict should things end up in a court of law.

These days, the cameras trained on crowds and monitored from state-of-the-art control rooms, many of which overlook the playing surface, have been supplemented by the increasing use of handheld cameras, to film crowds as they head to and from grounds, and the hoolivan, which provides not only additional cameras, but can also serve as a mobile control centre. The idea – and excuse – is to both deter hooligans and provide additional intelligence where possible.

The game has also witnessed the development of the photophone. This quite amazing system was used to incredible effect during Euro 96 (as I know to my cost, as I was stopped and photographed fifteen times over a period of three days), as it allows the instant exchange of information between the control centre and the officers on the ground, via an electronic mail network known as EPI. Aside from that, football has also been used to trial cameras in policemen's helmets, cameras fixed to dogs and horses and even listening devices placed under seats. The area around Millwall was also used to test a face-recognition computer system known as Mandrake.

These technological developments have been more than matched by the advancement in information and intelligence management. The original football unit was formed in 1989 to try and combat the growing problems associated with England fans abroad. This was absorbed into NCIS in 1990 and comprised of six full-time officers led by a superintendent. Although initially established in 1992 to combat serious and organised crime, the football section of NCIS not only provided a central co-ordinating point for the various FIOs around the country, but provided planning and intelligence for all overseas trips involving both England and club sides.

Key to the agency's success was its database. Astonishingly, by 1992 the unit had the details and photographs of over 6000 known or suspected hooligans on file and this grew with almost every single incident. Anyone involved or suspected of being involved in trouble was added, as was each and every individual arrested for a football-related offence abroad. Once on the system, people would be allocated a specific category, depending on the severity of the offence: category A (peaceful supporter), category B (possible risk of involvement in disorder) or category C (violent supporter or organiser of violence).

This information would be routinely exchanged with foreign police forces in accordance with a number of established bi-lateral agreements. As a result, NCIS had the option of applying for a domestic and international banning order for anyone either causing or becoming involved in trouble in those European states where agreements existed. Furthermore, NCIS was responsible for upholding certain European directives on spectator-related violence and the conviction of anyone charged with a football-related offence in England.

Although it has been widely known about in hooligan circles from day one, what really brought NCIS to the public's attention was Euro 96 and the huge operation to stop violence surrounding the first major tournament to be held in England since the 1966 World Cup. But it wasn't so much the success or even the size of the operation that caught the public eye, it was the cost. Initial rumours put the cost in the region of £10 million, but the true price was actually nearer £25 million, although seventy-five per cent of that was funded by the Football Trust.

For the first time people began to look seriously at what policing the game was costing. It was often quite a shock – Premier league clubs alone paid out £2.9 million to police the 1996–97 season – and that perception wasn't helped by some bizarre and very public admissions of failure. Three of the most high-profile of these were the riot in Dublin in 1995 when English supporters forced the abandonment of a friendly against the Republic of Ireland; the 1998 World Cup in France when the fans rioted in Marseille; and Euro 2000 and the disturbance at Charleroi.

Prior to all three occasions NCIS had stressed that it was way ahead of the game, which clearly wasn't the case. Indeed, on the morning after the riot in the South of France it publicly stated that hardly any of the large number of hooligans involved were known to them, although, to be fair, this riot was more a reaction to the way the locals were behaving than simple, bog-standard hooliganism. Similarly, in spite of a massive police operation to prevent trouble at the tournament, of 965 England fans arrested only one was subject to a football banning order and only thirty-five were known to NCIS as prominent football hooligans at all. While NCIS claimed that this was proof its operation to stop known hooligans from travelling was working, it couldn't hide the fact that this was a major embarrassment for the English police.

In spite of this, NCIS continued to forge ahead with its work and, to be fair, has enjoyed a huge amount of success, particularly in relation to the travelling England fans and the training of both foreign police and domestic stewards. It even took on the running of the Football Banning Orders Authority for England and Wales (FBOA) on behalf of the Home Office. In fact, so solid was its reputation that the agency has served as a model for the creation of similar anti-hooligan organisations in various countries across Europe. However, on 1 January 2006 NCIS was absorbed into the larger Serious Organised Crime Agency (SOCA) and prior to that happening it was decided that the football department would be better suited outside. As a result, both the national football intelligence function and FBOA were merged into a single dedicated unit, the UK Football Policing Unit (UK FPU).

This was charged with responsibility for all matters relating to policy and operational delivery, including the coordination of ports policing operations when required and the management of all funding for anti-hooligan operations, all of which had previously carried out by the Association of Chief Police Officers. It also took over the existing football intelligence role, as well as those duties previously undertaken by the FBOA.

Not surprisingly, with the World Cup on the horizon, the UK FPU was launched in a blaze of publicity. However, just to enhance its chances of success, prior to the 2005–06 season the Government tightened up the legislation relating to banning orders, thus ensuring that the figures went through the roof. Time will tell how effective the UK FPU will be, but having spoken to some of its senior staff, they are confident of success at least on the international stage. Indeed, both FIFA and UEFA have recently acknowledged the good work being done here on the anti-hooligan front.

Yet no matter how dedicated or efficient the police might be, they are only as effective as the legislation they have to work within. Luckily, of all the areas that have seen major changes in recent decades, the legal framework set in place to help the police deal with anyone who commits an offence at football is by far and away the most significant. It is also one of the most contentious.

In the early days, hooliganism was dealt with under normal bog-standard law in place to prosecute anyone causing bodily harm to another individual or criminal damage to property. However, the nightmare events that took place during 1985, and in particular the Bradford fire and the riot at St Andrews, finally forced the government into action.

The Justice Popplewell report into the fire was released in 1986 and focussed on the issue of supporter safety inside grounds. It also formed the basis of the 1989 Football Supporters Act, which handed the courts the power to award legally enforceable restriction orders to any fan convicted of a football-related offence. This not only stopped them attending games at home, but abroad as well, and was seen as a major victory for the police.

However, the other key recommendation in the act, the setting up of a compulsory national identity card scheme for supporters, was more problematic. Even before the act came to pass the Football League had agreed to set up such a scheme at all its professional clubs, but in the event only thirteen of the ninety-two actually bothered. Thankfully, despite strenuous backing from the then prime minister Margaret Thatcher, the entire thing was dropped in the wake of the Hillsborough disaster as being both unworkable and unwanted. In fact, the Lord Justice Taylor report into the tragedy equated the idea with 'using a sledgehammer to crack a nut'.

While a very positive and long overdue step in the right direction, just two years later the act was supplemented by the Football Offences Act 1991. This strengthened the law with regard to three specific areas: throwing missiles, invading the pitch and taking part in racist or indecent chanting.

A revised Football Disorder and Disorder Act was issued in 1999 which, among other things, made it clear that from that point forward the courts were actually required, not merely allowed, to make an international football banning order if the nature of the charges met certain criteria. Any fans handed a ban were also required to hand over their passports at a police station and report there at a specific time and date.

Also included in the act was the recommendation that anyone arrested for involvement in a football-related offence overseas should be charged and serve any subsequent sentence in the country where the offence took place. The problem was that despite this being an obligation of the European Convention on Spectator Violence and Misbehaviour at Sports, the vast majority of signatory countries merely rounded up and shipped out anyone who stepped out of line, much to the chagrin of NCIS.

In response to the trouble at Euro 2000, the act was amended again to combine both domestic and international banning orders. But, more importantly and controversially, it gave the courts the power to apply a banning order to an individual if the police lodged sufficient evidence with them to suggest that they had been involved in violence in the UK or elsewhere in the past and that there were 'reasonable' grounds to believe that a banning order would help prevent acts of hooliganism in the future.

With bans lasting anywhere from two to ten years, depending on the nature of the offence or complaint, so effective a weapon have they become (almost a thousand were issued in 2005 alone, bringing the total to almost 3500) that the police and the CPS strengthened the entire system even further at the beginning of the 2005–06 season by announcing that cooperation between the two groups would now become standard practice for all football-related cases. Furthermore, any case which passed a basic evidential test would almost certainly be pushed forward for prosecution rather than dropped. As a statement of intent, it was as good and public as they come, implying, as it did, that if the battle to defeat the hooligans hadn't been won, the end was certainly in sight – except it was all a distortion of the very unpalatable truth that, far from being over, domestically the war is still raging, while victory on the international stage might be in sight, but only largely thanks to the sterling work being done by the fans themselves to change our image abroad.

However, worse than that, the continuing drive to instil confidence in the performance of the police at football disguises some very unsavoury facts, many of which involve either misleading the public or simply abusing the power the police already have at their disposal. And while some might argue that this is nothing more than another case of 'well, he would say that,' the reality is that the evidence to support this thinking isn't too hard to find if you know where to look and what you're looking for. In fact, the most obvious place to start involves the annual arrest figures and what they tell us about what's been going on – or rather what they don't.

Interestingly, when these figures first began to come out, they included a brief account of the more serious incidents. This made for fascinating reading, so much so, in fact, that this was stopped when the police suddenly realised that the hooligans were actually quite keen for their clubs to feature and were widely ridiculed if they didn't!

These days, things are far more official, with the figures broken down into all kinds of categories and statistics before being released by NCIS in a blaze of publicity at the start of every new season. Invariably they are accompanied by some kind of claim along the lines of 'things are improving but we should not be complacent because of increasing concerns about some kind of new phenomenon which threatens the status quo'. In the past, this has included the notion that hard-core hooligans are funding their activities through organised crime, to an alarming increase in the number of teenage hooligans running with organised firms. Both of these assertions have an obvious shock value, but neither are new or particularly relevant to ninety-five per cent of lads who regularly play up at games, yet they were presented in such a way as to suggest that they were. However, it is the figures themselves which cause me problems or, more specifically, the way in which they are presented.

The figures for the 2004–05 season provide a case in point. The press release put out by the police the day before the numbers were unveiled was headed 'Soccer Thugs Crackdown Hailed' and went on to make the point that the number of banning orders handed out in the previous season had hit record levels. It then talked about an eleven per cent drop in arrests (to 3628) and the fact that only six people were arrested at overseas England and Wales internationals, before the obligatory quotes celebrating how well the police have been doing and then the warning against slacking off.

All good and encouraging stuff, but when you examine the actual figures things start to become a little confusing. One of the ways they are broken down is by the type of offence and of the 3628 people arrested only 1856 were detained for offences that can, as far as I am concerned, be legitimately tagged as being hooligan-related violence. These are public disorder (1428) and violent disorder (428). That leaves 1772, of which a further 314 individuals were arrested for offences which could be termed as being hooligan-related: possession of an offensive weapon (36), missile-throwing (76), breach of the peace (140) or breach of a banning order (62).

That's a total of 2170, which to me is the true arrest figure, as the remaining 1458 were charged with offences which have little or nothing to do with hooliganism at all. These included racist chanting (51), ticket-touting (146) and even 976 people arrested for offences relating to alcohol. Quite why they even appear on this document escapes me.

Things become even cloudier when you look at it from another angle, for of that 3628, 1491 were arrested actually inside a ground, which almost certainly rules out the vast majority of those 2170 people who were detained for anything to do with hooliganism and certainly those nicked for ticket-touting.

When one considers that in the 2004–05 season over 37 million people walked through a turnstile into an English football ground it seems to me that, given those figures, our stadia appear to be fairly safe places to visit. With an average of 1.21 arrests per game, even outside looks to be far safer than my local town centre on a Saturday night.

This begs two questions and which one you ask depends on what you know about the game and the issue of hooliganism. If you know very little and take the figures as read and in simple black and white, the fact that they are so low seems to indicate that hooliganism isn't anything like the major problem the police say it is. So in that case the question has to be asked, why the big fuss? After all, just over 2000 arrests per year is hardly value for money given the millions it costs to police the game.

However, if you know a bit more about football and attend matches on a regular basis, then the question you would have to ask is how come those figures don't seem to equate to what I see on a weekly basis? Because in all honesty, they don't. What they do, however, is disguise a simple truth, for while they might suggest to Mr and Mrs Average that things are improving, the only thing they really seem to prove is that the police don't arrest anyone anymore. At least not there and then. After all, anyone who has attended a major local derby or cup tie recently will know only too well that the threat of hooliganism continues to be a very real one and the police operations to combat that threat are often huge. For example, 300 officers were on duty for the Sheffield derby in February 2006, a game at which a number of policemen were injured during clashes between fans from both clubs.

Even small games at a relatively hooligan-free ground such as Watford's Vicarage Road are being overseen by numerous police patrolling in vans, on foot and even occasionally, on horseback, yet no matter how many police they have on duty, they will invariably be guided by someone in a control room with access to CCTV. And therein lies the problem, because the police increasingly rely on the use of cameras to help contain events on the ground, while using them to gather evidence to make any required arrests at a later date.

By approaching the problem in this incredibly time-consuming and expensive way, it is surely obvious that the number of arrests for actual acts of violence or aggression will be lower and even the police must realise that the lower they are, the fewer resources they will be able to demand. Could this, in part, explain why the figures for hooliganism are clearly padded out with the addition of 976 drunks?

Or is it, as some people argue, because they know that by keeping hooliganism out of the public eye on matchdays and in it through the use of high-profile early morning raids and court cases, they can continue to fuel the ongoing demonisation of the football hooligan? And by doing so, can exploit their existence to develop measures of control that might prove useful when dealing with other potentially more dangerous and volatile public order situations in the future?

That might seem a slightly fanciful notion, but given the attention the problem attracts, as well as the severity of the sentences handed out to anyone found guilty of a football-related offence – sentences which are wholly disproportionate to the nature and severity of the crime – then it makes a degree of sense. Even more so when one remembers that of all the areas of British society covered by the law of our land, football is just about the only one where the civil liberties groups refuse to tread. There are plenty of lads who have ended up in cells both here and abroad who will willingly testify to that.

The reason for this is fairly obvious in that, by its very nature, hooliganism is an illegal activity and, as such, is not only frowned upon by just about everyone, but is also one of those activities where people have been conditioned to feel that anyone caught and convicted deserves whatever comes their way. As a consequence, anyone wrongly arrested at football is, not to put too fine a point on it, up shit creek.

At the beginning of this chapter I highlighted the fact that to many lads the police are British football's biggest and most organised mob, but an addition to that is that they can never lose. After all, they have the law on their side, so how can they? What that means in real terms is that no matter what the circumstances, if the police say you are guilty, that chances are that no one with any degree of power or influence is going to take up your case for fear of it backfiring and making them look stupid. Hence, it's your word against theirs and in ninety-nine per cent of cases that means you lose.

Similarly, given that the police are so active in this area, even fewer in authority seem willing to question the tactics they choose to employ in the seemingly never-ending battle to defeat what has come to be accepted as one of society's great ills. This, in part, is how they have been able to blanket the nation with CCTV and place some of the most draconian and frightening restrictions on individual freedom ever seen in a civilised country on to the statute book without attracting barely a whimper of complaint. Then again, at a time when most people equate the term 'Big Brother' with a C4 reality TV show as opposed to the George Orwellian vision of the future, that shouldn't really be a surprise. After all, Orwell's future is already here in all but name and no one seems to care, if indeed they actually realise.

In respect of football, banning orders provide the best example of the kind of thing that is going on. For although they have proven to be incredibly effective, parts of the legislation governing their use borders on scandalous. Don't get me wrong. If someone steps out of line, breaks the law and is convicted in a court of law for a football-related offence, then I am all for seeing them banned from games for a period of time. To me, that is both a sensible and just punishment.

After all, no one has a divine right to walk into a football ground just because they are a football fan. I even accept and support the idea of stopping people subjected to legitimate banning orders from travelling abroad for international games. Why should the majority have to suffer from the presence of someone who may or may not become a problem at some point?

However, I have a major problem with the idea of those same 'sentences', for that is what they are, being imposed on people who have not been convicted of anything. Indeed, I find the idea that someone can have their passport taken off them and be banned from a certain area of their own homeland simply because the police 'think' they might be a problem absolutely abhorrent and so should every right-thinking person in this land. This is, after all, a democratic country not a third world dictatorship. Or at least it was the last time I looked.

The fact that the police can make these assumptions based on so-called evidence dating back up to ten years is bad enough, but when one considers that even unwitting association with known hooligans could theoretically be enough to put someone before a court and potentially remove one of the most basic of human rights – the right to travel across borders – then that is simply frightening, and even more so when one considers that the chances of winning any appeal are almost certainly zero.

However, what really galls me about this is that I simply cannot understand why the police even need this legislation at all. Surely, given the resources, manpower and time they have at their disposal, if they suspect that someone is involved in what is after all a crime, they should be able to prove it? But now, of course, they don't have to, and now those laws are on the books not only will we as a society never be rid of them, but it is only a matter of time before their use spreads into other areas of both criminal and not-so-criminal activity to provide what amounts to state control over the individual. That, if anything, shows a major miscalculation by the various civil liberties groups, which only voiced half-hearted criticism when those laws were first mooted.

Sadly, the banning order system is not the only area of the law relating to football to cause concern, not just to me, but to fans the length and breadth of the country, because the behaviour of some of the officers who police our game is occasionally less than acceptable.

It is important to remember, however, that even the most active of hooligans has always accepted that the authorities are duty-bound to uphold the rule of law. The problem, in part, lies in how they apply that law, because often that isn't so clear cut and in too many instances certainly isn't fair. Anyone who has spent years following their club knows only too well that certain police forces are more tolerant than others, while some aren't tolerant at all.

To be fair, this is understandable to a degree. Policing games must be an incredibly daunting experience on occasions and I have spoken to enough coppers over the years to know that a good number of them are quite anti football fans, particularly lads, but there are also plenty more who get a huge buzz out of the thrill of the chase and the ongoing competition with the football mobs. After all, if you look at it objectively they get pretty much the same experiences in terms of excitement and they get paid for the privilege. That said, on occasions it must also be incredibly boring and so it's little wonder that once in a while, some of them like to poke a stick into the hornets' nest to see what happens.

So just what do the police get up to in their ongoing battle with the Saturday lads? Well, it is fair to say that were the desire there I could easily fill another book with instances of abuses of power, simple assaults and even basic rudeness aimed at football fans in general, let alone active hooligans, but the bottom line is that in their desire to control, contain and occasionally antagonise the violent minority, the police are not afraid to adopt some very unorthodox spoiling tactics.

In the main, these will be designed to achieve a variety of things, from keeping one group apart from another through to restricting the numbers who actually travel. However, most will be used simply to let lads know that Old Bill is on their case and show them that if they step out of line, they'll get hammered.

Possibly the most frequently used is Section 60, a part of the 1994 Criminal Justice and Public Order act which permits the stopping and searching of anyone believed to have either been, or is likely to become, involved with acts of violence. Although the rules to authorise the use of Section 60 are quite clear, the implementation of them is often confusing in so much as it is not unknown for officers to stop and search people when the use of those powers have not yet been authorised. It is also not unknown for the police to exceed their powers under Section 60 and take names and addresses or search wallets, neither of which they are actually permitted to do.

For anyone not familiar with the process, this can be a daunting and even frightening experience. However, most in-the-know lads are well aware of the rules governing the use of a Section 60, so they know exactly what is and isn't allowed. They also know that pushing your luck when stopped invariably means a risk of increased hassle, so they stay quiet and simply let the police get on with things.

Occasionally, the stop and search will be supplemented by the use of Section 30 of the Anti-Social Behaviour Act. This gives police the power to disperse groups of two or more from a designated area and provides an officer with the power to arrest anyone who returns to an area from which they have previously been dispersed – an invaluable tool for clearing an area quickly.

Yet while Section 60 can be applied to both home and away fans, by far the most usual method of exerting their power is the way the police deal with travelling fans. It is, for example, reasonably standard practice these days for the police to stop coaches they suspect are full of lads and hold them somewhere, such as a lay-by or a service station, for a while. This tactic not only stops the lads from getting a drink before the game, but puts the block on them meeting up with anyone else.

Similarly, when games have the potential for disorder it is becoming increasingly common for the police to insist that only fans travelling on official coaches should be able to purchase tickets for the game. In some instances, those tickets will only be actually handed over while en route. This is a relatively simple way of restricting numbers, as well as identifying and controlling everyone who travels.

And it isn't just coach travel which is subject to such attention. Train travellers are frequently inconvenienced on their way to and from games by being held on platforms – often without any information about what is happening or how long you will be held – or on trains, which are simply pulled into sidings. Again, this can be for hours, depending on the mood of the local police, and can be incredibly frustrating, although to be fair, the British Transport police often have good reason to deal harshly with football fans. For example, the network saw a massive rise in incidents during the 2004–05 season, with over 332 taking place, of which sixty-two were deemed serious. There were also 292 arrests.

Even when you arrive at a ground policing can sometimes be extremely oppressive and I've seen far too many examples of coppers herding fans along as if they were cattle and closing pubs after games simply because they want people out of their town or city.

Air travellers are also targets for attention, especially when attempting to travel to international games. Here, the search for anyone trying to avoid the restriction of a banning order is aided by the existence of the Football Disorder Act, which allows police to detain anyone they suspect could be travelling to cause trouble for up to six hours at the airport while they check into their background. This means supporters can often be seen being dragged out of queues and ritually embarrassed in front of everyone else in the terminal.

Interestingly, the police also have the power to issue a temporary order banning individuals from travelling if they have firm reasons for suspecting they are potential hooligans. This could lead to a formal court ban if it ends up in court.

I have also heard of numerous cases where lads have been held up so they miss their flights and even instances where supporters have been questioned and released, only to find that when they get to the check-in, the airlines refuse to carry them having been given the nod that they are suspected football hooligans.

I could go on here, but I'm sure you get the point that the police aren't above bending the law to get the job done. To be fair, most lads accept that as being par for the course and when problems do occur, it is usually because 'normal' fans get caught up in things and take exception to the way they have been treated.

Of course that is when they, just like everyone else, realise that as a football fan, especially a travelling football fan, you have no right of either complaint or redress. As a visiting supporter no local copper is ever going to be interested in anything you have to say about a fellow officer policing a game and that assumes that you would be prepared to hang around long enough to even try and find one. Equally, a complaint made at your local station would soon be lost under a mountain of paperwork and confusion. So, with no organisation to call them to account and no real body willing to deal with complaints relating to football matters, the police have been handed pretty much carte blanche to do whatever they like – within reason of course.

While understandable to an extent, one has to wonder why this situation has been allowed not only to develop, but also to continue, especially since it has an obvious knock-on and negative effect in terms of the public's perception of the police. Continue it does, though, and quite for how long goodness only knows. Indeed, just what the future holds for the policing of the game is unclear. I cannot for the life of me believe that the Old Bill will ask for any more legislation, especially since on 1 January 2006 they were handed the power to arrest anyone committing any offence on the spot! (Previously, they were only able to do that for offences which carried a sentence of at least five years in prison.)

However, it is clear that, like much of what has already gone on, new developments will be driven by technology. Already, during the build-up to the 2006 World Cup, we have seen the Dutch police send 17,000 text messages to the mobile phones of fans who attended the 2004–05 match between local rivals Feyenoord and Ajax asking for information about the ringleaders of the serious trouble which took place at the game. As a direct result, five people eventually handed themselves in.

Furthermore, the German Government intends to use biometric face recognition systems to identify known trouble-makers at the tournament and it will also employ a new mobile optical fingerprint system for fast identification based on data for people with a criminal record. There are even plans for the Germans to utilise AWAC early warning aircraft to track the movements of hooligans travelling across the borders and around the country. I'm not sure we'll go as far as to have military aircraft flying over grounds here, but certainly the electronic and remote identification of individuals is something the police in this country are keen to develop further. But whatever happens, it is clear to me that something has to be done to try and strike a balance between the need to deal with the hooligan threat and the wishes of the general public, because on too many occasions, that balance is not being struck.

I opened this chapter by discussing the reasons why it would be useful to see a book examining the hooliganism issue from a police perspective and mentioned a couple of reasons why we may never see it. But another reason is that, increasingly, like many people who commentate on this issue, I have come to believe that, over the years, the existence of hooliganism as a problem has been of huge benefit to the police. This is primarily because the continued lack of understanding about the root causes of it have allowed them to exploit the sport I love for their own ends, often at the expense of law-abiding fans who not only deserve but demand better. So why would they want to talk openly about that?

This is not an opinion I am proud of, nor is it one I am glad to hold. It is nevertheless a product of years of negative experiences, some of which were outlined in *Barmy Army*, along with a few more that were provided by people who, like me, have witnessed abuses of position and power that go way beyond anything one should ever expect from someone charged with upholding the law of the land. Unfortunately, nothing I have seen or heard in the five years since *Barmy Army* was first published has caused me to change that opinion. Indeed, if anything, I have become even more jaundiced. The reason, quite simply, is the police's attitude, not just to football lads, but to football in general. To be blunt, I think it sucks.

The fact that in most instances the police are never held to account is bad enough, but what really causes me problems is that after decades of policing football, they are seemingly always chasing more – be it money, resources, technology or even legislation – and, invariably, they are given it, usually without question.

Equally importantly, while the majority of fans welcome the success they are having at the moment in terms of reducing trouble overseas, the fact remains that this success is totally false. It is, after all, based not on conviction rates, but on legislation which is quite simply disgraceful. Furthermore, in terms of solving the problem domestically, while I do not accept that this is wholly a police responsibility, there can be little doubt that all anyone is achieving at the moment is keeping a lid on things. The reality is that any kind of solution is as far away as it has ever been. Given the millions of pounds and hours spent on this problem over the years, that is simply not good enough. Football, and most importantly, those who follow and fund the game, deserve better. Much better.

CHAPTER SEVEN
ECHELON

In the previous chapter I examined the role of the police at football and touched on their increasing use of technology. However, one thing I neglected to discuss, at least not at any length, was the use of phone tapping, mail interception, text tracing and internet and email monitoring.

There was a good reason for that, because of all the issues surrounding hooliganism and the police, this one has proven all but impossible to examine with any degree of accuracy. We all suspect it goes on, of course. In fact, most people are sure it does. But no one can really prove it. After all, the Old Bill are hardly likely to put their hands up and admit it, so all I can do here is to talk about my own experiences and put forward theories about what I suspect goes on.

For example, when I started writing about this subject and became more critical of the authorities, I always suspected that sooner or later my phone would be tapped. Eventually, I discovered it had been, when a policeman actually stopped me and quoted something from a phone call I'd had that very morning.

Similarly, prior to Euro 96, suspicions were aroused that mail being sent to the post office box I had was being tampered with or simply stopped altogether. As a consequence, to test this out I had a number of letters sent to me from around the country by lads I knew and trusted. I even posted some to myself. About twenty-five per cent of these failed to arrive. Not conclusive proof admittedly, but enough to cause concern.

As time passed and I became more adept at using the internet, it became fairly obvious that the police were monitoring various hooligan-related websites, because not only would rogue posts appear from time to time, asking for information about this or that, but incidents that had been set up were invariably broken up by the police before anything could occur. However, what really proved it to me was something that happened back in 2001.

I had been contacted by a lad whose son was autistic and, as anyone who knows about such things will understand, kids who suffer from that terrible disease often have something on which they fixate. The kiddie who lives next door to me, for example, is obsessed with trains and so his parents often have to take him to working steam museums to provide him with his fix. However, in this case the lad concerned collected enamel football badges and so I was asked if I'd be able to get him any. I immediately sent what I had, badgered various football people into supplying a load more and put out a request on a number of the hoolie boards.

The Saturday after, I was walking away from a game at Vicarage Road when I heard a shout. I turned to see a policeman in full uniform running at me, so stopped to see what he wanted. He simply said, 'Alright Doug, I've got something for you from the lads at the nick,' and pulled out a bag full of badges. As proof, that's really as good as it gets.

Of course, other things are more difficult to check and we can only make assumptions based on what we read about things which happen around other areas of criminal activity. It is well known, for example, that the mobile phone companies are happy to work with the police on all manner of crimes, as evidenced by the Dutch hooligans being contacted via text messaging, and so there are plenty of lads involved with hooliganism who have a dedicated and anonymous pay-as-you-go phone they use at football, which they are happy to throw away if the Old Bill come anywhere near.

Equally, I have certainly heard rumours that messenger services of the type run by AOL and Microsoft have been monitored in the past to try and capture paedophiles, while the aftermath of the terrorist attacks on 7 July 2005 highlighted just how sophisticated the police are in tracking individuals through the use of CCTV and mobile phone and email tracking. Is it really so hard to believe that, given the seriousness with which they treat football hooliganism, much the same thing doesn't go on around this?

Indeed, it was exactly that thinking which eventually led me to develop a conspiracy theory surrounding football. It is somewhat complicated, but the more I thought about it, the more it made sense. So much so in fact, that eventually I wrote it up as a potential novel. It's called *Echelon*, but sadly, for a variety of reasons, it remains unwritten. However, while the story and its characters are entirely fictitious, it encapsulates certain things many people have come to suspect about the role of the police at football and I've included it here simply because, if nothing else, it will get you thinking – or at least it should.

When the National Criminal Intelligence Service (NCIS) releases a report suggesting that organised crime is behind an apparent increase in football hooliganism, 27-year-old freelance investigative television journalist Pete Hutchinson is contacted by BBC producer Keith Haynes and asked if he wants to film an exposé of the thugs involved at one of the clubs named in the report, Tottenham Hotspur.

Intrigued by the idea, Hutchinson carries out some initial research and, after discussing it at length with Haynes, agrees to go undercover to try to discover the types of crime the hooligans are involved with. The ultimate aim is to produce a hard-hitting documentary and then hand his evidence to the police, allowing them to secure convictions.

Initially, he begins by attending games at White Hart Lane and gradually becomes a familiar figure among the home supporters both inside the ground and in the various pubs outside. So much so that, within a few months, he is on first name terms with Dave Mason, the publican of the Old Bank on Seven Sisters Road and is regularly invited to attend away games with some of the more vocal lads. However, when they travel, trouble is never far away and Hutchinson not only finds himself becoming involved in occasional violence, but, thanks to a pinhole camera, he is able to capture huge amounts of footage on film, including acts carried out by some of the hard-core ringleaders at the club.

Yet despite becoming increasingly familiar to some of them, after six months' work he is still no nearer infiltrating the central hooligan hard-core as their natural suspicion of relative newcomers continues to make any kind of connection seem impossible. And when the little research he is able to do begins to suggest that there is no real evidence to support the claims made in the police report, he begins to dismiss it as nothing more than a PR exercise for NCIS.

However, rather than change direction and investigate that, he decides to cut his losses and get out, a choice made all the easier when his girlfriend Joanne, a senior researcher at Sky News, announces that she is pregnant and asks him to give up his potentially dangerous occupation. He promises Joanne that he will tell Keith Haynes that very evening as the two of them have been invited to attend a reception at the BBC and Haynes is one of the hosts.

Haynes' reaction to the news is unexpected. Initially, he is furious, but then he seems almost relieved. However, he demands that Hutchinson meet him to discuss it further the very next day. Although taken aback by the reaction, Hutchinson agrees.

Later that evening, Joanne meets a man whom she introduces to Hutchinson as David Galvin. A freelance producer who has just started working for BskyB, Galvin claims to recognise Hutchinson and is certain the two of them had worked together on a programme some years before. Despite not remembering him at all, in typical media fashion Hutchinson simply feigns recognition and the two of them are soon making small talk. As they chat, Galvin asks Hutchinson what he has been doing since their last meeting, but when he is loath to respond with any detail, Galvin swiftly moves the conversation along. By the time the evening draws to a close, the two of them are talking and acting like old friends.

Next morning, Hutchinson visits Haynes to discuss the decision to shelve the project. However, when Hutchinson enters the producer's office he is surprised to find him in the company of a man who introduces himself as Detective Inspector Jim Bailey of NCIS. He tells Hutchinson that Keith Haynes had been keeping NCIS informed about the documentary idea from day one and they are disappointed to hear that the project is to be shelved, for in their opinion it has the potential both to secure the conviction of some of Europe's most notorious hooligans and provide a way of sending a clear message to those intent on causing trouble at football.

Indeed, so keen are they on the idea that Bailey has come to offer any assistance they can in the hope that Hutchinson will reconsider his decision. Hearing this, Hutchinson asks for twenty-four hours to think it through, as well as discuss it with Joanne.

As he leaves the BBC after the meeting, Hutchinson is amazed to literally collide with a still hungover David Galvin. The two of them exchange pleasantries about the night before and then, out of the blue, Galvin offers Hutchinson a job on a documentary series he has just had commissioned. However, Hutchinson immediately turns him down, adding excitedly that a project he had thought was dead in the water has just been given new life.

The next morning, having spoken with Joanne, Hutchinson calls Haynes and tells him he will return to work on the hooligan project, but only for three months. If by then he has made no progress, he will stop work on it for good.

From that point on, Bailey starts supplying Hutchinson with classified information supporting the NCIS report, but he supplements that help with advice about infiltration, key to which is the assertion that no one would ever get fully accepted by a hooligan firm simply by going to football and hanging around them. Hooliganism simply doesn't work like that. The only way in, at least according to Bailey, is to earn their respect as a fighter. That would take years of proving yourself by scrapping at games the length and breadth of the country and, clearly, Hutchinson doesn't have that time, so Bailey tells him that there is one other way. However, before he tells him what it is, he would need to know how far Hutchinson would be prepared to go to get his story. When Hutchinson tells him that he will go as far as it takes, Bailey smiles and then asks if he would be prepared to break the law. Intrigued, Hutchinson simply repeats the fact that he would do whatever he had to.

On hearing this, Bailey tells him that, given his time constraints, the only way he will ever get inside the gang is by integrating himself into their lifestyle. In short, he has to become directly involved with their criminal activities. Before Hutchinson can answer, Bailey offers to help him become involved in those activities in return for enough evidence to convict one man – Gary Taylor, the man regarded as the leader of the Tottenham group and someone Bailey has been after for years.

Hutchinson is stunned at the suggestion. However, Bailey explains that this had been standard practice in the past, but because of increased fears about undercover officers being caught on camera indulging in criminal activity, the police have been forced to abandon it. As a result, hooligan-related convictions have fallen off, while criminal activity surrounding it has increased. Hutchinson's involvement has come at the perfect time for NCIS, because the fact that he is a journalist means that, should anything go wrong, any potential repercussions wouldn't be so great.

Despite his own reservations, Hutchinson asks how the arrange-ment would work. Bailey then hands him a folder containing informa-tion on Taylor and two other members of the Tottenham hooligan gang he has been trying to infiltrate. The information implicates them in various criminal activities, ranging from protection to large-scale car crime, but Bailey adds that the police are increasingly concerned that the three are looking to move into the importation of drugs from Holland. Because of that, he would be willing to supply Hutchinson with quantities of cocaine and ecstasy for him to trade with them and therefore establish an almost unquestionable and instant credibility. He would, of course, escape any kind of prosecution, because if he did build a case against the three, it would be based on the targets' existing criminal activities, not any possible future ones. And with careful editing of the documentary, no-one need ever even know how he managed to work his way in. Hutchinson is astounded, but, mindful of the fact that if the police are willing to go to such lengths to obtain convictions, this must be a huge story, he accepts Baileys offer.

Within weeks, he has begun to supply pills and cocaine to lads on the peripheries of the gang and is soon being invited to spend time with them outside of matchdays. However, this begins to have an increasing impact on his relationship with Joanne who, fearful for his safety and ignorant of the operation he is involved with, begins to exert more and more pressure on him to get out and leave it all behind, reminding him that within a few months he's going to be a father with all the responsibilities that entails. Despite her concerns, he remains driven by a desire to get the story and so continues. And, with his credibility seemingly assured as a result of his dealing activities, is eventually introduced to Gary Taylor.

However, things do not go as Hutchinson expects, for while Taylor occasionally indulges in a small amount of cocaine use on matchdays, it quickly becomes clear to Hutchinson that he has no interest in becoming any kind of supplier at all, which is something that does not fit in with the information Bailey had given him. Furthermore, Hutchinson soon begins to realise that the only thing any of the hard-core are seemingly guilty of is involvement in the planning and execution of football violence. Away from the game, they are apparently normal men who lead relatively normal lives. Hooliganism is just something they do at weekends, because they get a huge buzz from it. Bewildered by this apparent contradiction, Hutchinson begins to wonder if he will ever get his documentary completed.

However, when a neighbour's flat is burgled and it takes almost twelve hours for a policeman to appear, he suddenly realises that something odd is going on, for while policemen on the beat are increasingly rare, at most of the games he attends there are hundreds of them. Yet despite that, lads who cause trouble week in and week out, more often than not in full view of the police, are still walking around apparently without a care in the world. Indeed, the police are even having to use Hutchinson himself to gain evidence against a man who is clearly guilty of extreme acts of violence. Why?

Fascinated by this idea, Hutchinson starts to think about the whole issue of hooliganism from another perspective and, for the first time, begins to wonder if some of the rumours he has heard about the police during his time among the hooligans might actually be true. After all, he has seen enough during his time with Taylor to know that plenty of policemen regard football duty as nothing more than either a stress release or a way to extract revenge against the general public.

So, during the journey to a game at Southampton, he raises the issue with the other lads and is amazed at their response. Stories of police brutality come flooding out and he is even told of at least one force which is known for delivering punishment beatings to known hooligans rather than dragging them into court if they are arrested. When Gary Taylor joins them and hears what they're talking about, he bursts out laughing and makes the point that as far as he's concerned, the police are the biggest hooligan firm in the country. After all, there are plenty of them, they have all the resources they could ever possibly need and they have the law on their side. More importantly, they are all but unaccountable for their actions. Even if someone does bother to make a complaint, who is going to believe a suspected hooligan over a policeman?

Listening to them, Hutchinson is shocked at the matter-of-fact way they talk about what is potentially a major civil liberties issue. Increasingly disturbed, and without mentioning anything to Bailey, he begins to research the role of the police at football and especially the amount of money and technology that they have at their disposal. He is astonished at some of the things he finds, for not only do they have access to seemingly limitless funding, but they have cutting-edge surveillance technology that is being used without any apparent accountability or, more significantly, results.

It is during this research that he stumbles across a report into Echelon. This is a top-secret, intelligence-gathering system developed by NASA for use as an anti-terrorist weapon, which has, in effect, become Big Brother. Not only is it able to intercept every single form of communication known to man, it has the capability to track the movements of targeted individuals to within yards, no matter where they are on the planet. When he reads that the system is triggered by the use of key words, such as terrorist or bomb, and that the system is rumoured to incorporate one of the most powerful face-recognition systems yet devised, the hairs on the back of Hutchinson's head stand on end, because face recognition is one of the key weapons NCIS cites as vital in its battle against the hooligans. Having read that, Hutchinson begins to suspect that English football crowds, and in particular hooligan gangs, are unwittingly being used as guinea pigs in the development of Echelon.

The more he thinks about it and the more he reads, the more obvious it is. After all, where better to carry out both the development and the operational training than at football? Where else in the world do you get groups of men using all kinds of communications to plan criminal activities at least once every week? This would also go some way towards explaining why so few of the high-profile hooligan ringleaders have been convicted over the last few years. Quite simply, NASA needs them on the street.

Hutchinson realises that if he is right, that work must be being done with the full knowledge and consent of everyone from the people who run the game right through to government and the security services. The only people who don't know are the fans themselves.

It then strikes him that if football is aware of what is going on, football must also be getting paid. And that, in turn, must be how and why so many English football clubs have continued to exist, despite having balance sheets that show huge debts running into millions of pounds. What if those debts didn't really exist at all? After all, they could hardly have a steady stream of income from NASA showing in the accounts, but the money would have to be hidden somewhere.

With his head spinning at what, on the face of it, is a huge conspiracy theory that actually stands up to examination, Hutchinson is at a loss as to what to do next. He knows that his original project is all but dead in the water thanks to a lack of supporting evidence, but is also aware that, potentially, he has a world-class story on his hands. Initially, he runs his theory past David Galvin, who has become a close friend of both his and Joanne, because he is aware that, as a fellow producer, Galvin will be able to offer some insight into how best to proceed. Galvin is stunned and excited in equal measures, so much so that he offers to help Hutchinson with the story in any way he can. However, like a true journalist, Hutchinson knows that before anything happens he has to speak to Keith Haynes, as only he can give him the authority to proceed.

That very afternoon, Hutchinson visits Keith Haynes and asks if he can scrap the hooligan project and run with the Echelon idea. Haynes is shocked at this development and asks to view all the videotapes Hutchinson has made, so that he can make a decision. However, with nothing much to show him, Hutchinson stalls and instead presses for a decision.

At 6 a.m. the very next morning, Hutchinson is lying in bed with Joanne when the police raid his house. Every shred of research is seized, before he is arrested and charged with involvement in organised football hooliganism and drug dealing. Both charges that his own tapes help support.

At the police station, an incredulous Hutchinson protests his innocence and when he is finally interviewed, he refers the arresting officers to DI Jim Bailey at NCIS. However, he is stunned when he is told that there is no officer of that name working at either NCIS or anywhere else. Things go from bad to worse when his producer Keith Haynes is interviewed by the police and denies any knowledge of Hutchinson's work, with the result that he is placed on remand and sent to jail.

Staggered by what has happened to him, Hutchinson begins to realise that not only has he been set up, but that he almost certainly has no way out. More worryingly, he has no real idea why, although with Haynes continuing to deny any knowledge of his project and the police seemingly unwilling to investigate anything that would help him, he is fairly certain that things will get worse before they get better. This is a worry that comes home with a vengeance when, on the strength of video and photographic evidence seized from his flat, Gary Taylor is also arrested and placed in the cell next to him.

Not surprisingly, an enraged Taylor has learnt who and what Hutchinson is and within days corners the journalist. Hutchinson pleads innocence and tries to explain to Taylor exactly what has happened and how they have both been set up, but Taylor laughs off his story and beats Hutchinson to a pulp.

The next morning, as he recovers in the prison hospital, Hutchinson receives a visit from Joanne who tells him that following a break-in on her car and the theft of a box of master tapes, she has been sacked from her job as a researcher at Sky News for gross incompetence. More worryingly, her handbag was also stolen and her bank accounts emptied. When Hutchinson tells her he will transfer money from his accounts, he is stunned to discover that all of his assets have been frozen pending trial. He is, after all, on remand for alleged drug dealing.

His lack of funds not only heaps more stress on the heavily pregnant Joanne, it also means that he has to rely on a lawyer appointed for him by the court. However, she is hardly any use at all, especially as, other than Haynes and Bailey, the only two people who know anything about his hooligan project are Joanne and David Galvin, neither of whom have any real proof to support what he was doing.

With no one else to call upon, Hutchinson begins to wonder how he will ever prove his innocence. Increasingly convinced that the break-in to Joanne's car and her subsequent sacking were the work of Bailey, Haynes or whoever else set him up, and were designed solely to put added pressure on her and therefore him, he also begins to wonder if he is willing to let his girlfriend go through the ordeal of testifying on his behalf, especially since she will almost certainly be subjected to a gruelling cross-examination that will probably have little or no effect on an outcome that seems cut and dried.

Increasingly depressed by what is happening to him and certain that he has no way out, he decides to save her and plead guilty to all charges in the hope that he will get a reduced sentence. But when he leaves hospital and returns to his cell, he is shocked to discover that Gary Taylor has been released, apparently due to a lack of evidence.

Bewildered by this change of direction, Hutchinson suddenly realises that this is yet another ploy being used against him, for if his tapes had been used to establish Taylor's guilt, it would have helped lend some credibility to his own story when he had eventually come to court.

As a result, Hutchinson decides to go on the offensive. First he changes his plea to not guilty and then, sure in the knowledge that he will be convicted anyway, he uses his solicitor, Joanne and David Galvin to try and galvanise support among some of his more trusted journalist colleagues. The aim is to expose the truth behind what has happened once he has had his day in court. Unsurprisingly, few show any sign of helping him out, but following a chance remark from the prison governor, Hutchinson becomes suspicious that not only are all his letters and calls being monitored, but so are Joanne's and his solicitor's. He becomes convinced that this has far more to do with his ideas about Echelon than it does about hooliganism and drugs. He is also certain that what answers there are lie with the mysterious DI Jim Bailey.

From that point on, each letter Hutchinson sends and every phone call he makes includes a postscript asking Bailey to visit him, a ploy that eventually pays off when a week later he is taken to the visitors' block and finds Bailey waiting for him.

Hutchinson sits down and asks Bailey to tell him the truth about what happened. He is almost relieved to discover that Bailey's name is actually Michael Cowan and that he is an agent from MI5. Cowan confirms Hutchinson's suspicion that almost everything he told Haynes about Echelon is correct, but because the development of the system was ongoing, it has to be kept secret from the public. Anything else would obviously be against the long-term interests of both national and international security and simply could not be allowed.

When Hutchinson asks him why he allowed him to become involved in the first place, Cowan calmly replies that it was a simple exercise. Normally, if anyone from the media began sniffing around anything to do with Echelon, MI5 would simply exert pressure on the relative company executives to get them to pull away. But in this instance, he had decided to see how close to the truth someone could actually get. It was just a case of finding the right person.

When he had learnt that Keith Haynes was under investigation for VAT fraud, he had offered to have things 'sorted' in return for Haynes' help in finding a suitable candidate. Haynes had suggested Hutchinson, but the truth was that no documentary was ever going to be shown and the plug was always going to be pulled as soon as he even threatened to get too close to the truth. Indeed, Hutchinson had been under close-quarter surveillance from day one just to make sure he didn't.

The trouble was, when they had discovered what he suspected, as well as what he wanted to do, it had shocked them into action, because they hadn't realised how far he had gone. The consequence was that Hutchinson had to be taken out of circulation for a while until they were sure that they had recovered everything he had filmed or written, which they now were.

On hearing this Hutchinson is outraged and tells Cowan that he made copies of all his tapes and has hidden them somewhere they will never be found, but Cowan just laughs and tells him that even if he has, he would never dare use them. After all, it had only taken one phone call to have him arrested and thrown in jail. Does he really think it would be any more difficult to have him disappear altogether?

Hutchinson grudgingly admits that he is right and asks Cowan what is going to happen next. Cowan thinks for a moment and then replies simply that it is up to him. He can either sign the Official Secrets

Act, keep what he knows to himself and be released, or he can rot in prison, mouth off and have things tough. Either way, MI5 were going to be all over him like a rash for the rest of his life.

With release suddenly an option and the birth of his child imminent, Hutchinson takes the easy way out and within hours leaves prison a free man. Waiting at the gate for him is David Galvin, other than Joanne, the only person he feels able to trust. Yet when Galvin asks how and why his friend has suddenly been set free, Hutchinson simply remarks that he doesn't want to know.

As they are driving home, Hutchinson sits in silence and stares out of the window. For the first time, he is aware of just how easy it is to keep track of people in modern day Britain, be it through the numerous cameras watching him as he passes through the city or via satellite monitoring of the cell phone in David Galvin's car. He shudders visibly and sinks into his seat, but as he does so, a wry smile creeps across his face.

Six months later, just-married Peter and Joanne Hutchinson are sitting in their living room with their baby son when the phone rings. Peter answers it to find David Galvin on the line and as the two chat Peter decides that now the time is right to begin the battle to rebuild his reputation. However, mindful of the fact that his phone might be tapped, he asks Galvin to meet him for a drink the following afternoon.

Next day, Hutchinson and Galvin head off to a pub well away from the city. When they arrive, they settle in the garden and for the first time Hutchinson tells Galvin about the mysterious Michael Cowan and the involvement of MI5. Galvin is stunned and asks Hutchinson what he intends to do?

Hutchinson turns to Galvin and tells him that, with help, he intends to make a documentary to expose the truth behind Echelon and what has been going on right under the noses of the British public. Galvin is shocked and points out that, without any evidence, they would never be able to make anything, simply because they have no proof.

On hearing this, Hutchinson smiles and replies that he has proof. Tapes, photographs, everything they would need, all hidden away where no-one would ever suspect. Galvin is beside himself, but instinctively warns Hutchinson that it would be a huge risk if he tried to take on MI5, NASA and HM Government – a risk he might not be prepared to take. Hutchinson tells his friend that he understands his reluctance, but asks him to look over some of the evidence before he makes a decision. Again, Galvin voices his reluctance and urges Hutchinson to forget what has happened and move on, but Hutchinson is dead-set on proceeding and eventually convinces Galvin to examine what he has.

The next day a nervous Hutchinson arrives at Galvin's flat and hands him a CD-Rom. When they run it on Galvin's computer, it shows pictures, MPegs and even scanned documents. There is even a short MPeg of Michael Cowan taken in Keith Haynes' office with a hidden camera. Galvin studies it intently before asking how much more Hutchinson has. When he discovers that Hutchinson has copies of everything MI5 took from him, Galvin takes the CD ROM from the computer and hands it back before asking Hutchinson why he had never used any of this to secure his release from prison. But Hutchinson replies that he had no way of getting to it from inside a cell and did not want to involve anyone else directly. Besides, he had always believed that somehow, he would get out of prison and eventually, the truth would out.

Galvin shakes his head and tells Hutchinson that he wants nothing to do with it. It is simply too big and too dangerous. Furthermore, he pleads with Hutchinson to drop it, if only because his son needs a father. Hutchinson turns to leave, but not before telling Galvin that with or without his help, he will expose the truth. As a journalist, it is his duty.

As the door closes behind him, Galvin slumps into his chair and buries his head in his hands. Behind him, a second door opens and Michael Cowan steps out. He places a hand on Galvin's shoulder and thanks him for all his efforts. However, since they haven't worked and Hutchinson is hell-bent on going public, he has left them with no choice. After telling Galvin to take some leave and then report for reassignment, Cowan takes out a cell phone and dials.

A month later, Gary Taylor is sitting in the bar of the Old Bank reading a copy of the *Sun* when he happens across a story about a former BBC journalist who has been found dead in his car. The article then goes on to explain how the police are treating the death as suicide since the journalist concerned had recently been suffering from severe depression as a consequence of a recent spell in prison and the subsequent loss of his career. Taylor laughs out loud when he reads that the journalist was Peter Hutchinson and proceeds to show the story to the lads in the pub. As the paper circulates, Dave Mason takes hold of it and reads it carefully. Stunned to discover that his former patron had been a journalist, and that Taylor had ended up in prison because of him, he shocks everyone when he disappears into the back room and returns with two dusty but carefully sealed cardboard boxes. He places them on the counter and tells the lads that Hutchinson had left them with him for safekeeping months ago.

When Taylor asks him what is inside, Mason shrugs his shoulders, but adds that Hutchinson had actually visited him a few weeks back to take something out of one of them. Naturally curious, the lads ponder what the boxes contain, but general opinion is that they are full of drugs. After all, he had been supplying them for a while.

Suddenly, one of the lads grabs a box and, despite Mason's protests, tears it open to reveal a selection of photographs and videotapes. Each one carefully timed and dated. Seeing himself on some of the pictures, Taylor spreads a selection across the bar and stares at them for a second. Then, remembering what Hutchinson had told him in prison, he slowly raises his eyes to the small CCTV camera fitted to the wall above the bar. Without taking his eyes off it, he simply says 'Here Dave, what's the deal with that bloody camera then?'

PART THREE
RACISM

Whenever I talk or write anything about racism, the first thing that enters my head is a brief flash of a photograph or, to be more precise, a specific photograph of John Barnes – one of the greatest players ever to pull on a Watford shirt, let alone an England one, and one of the first players I ever truly idolised.

The picture, taken at the Merseyside derby in 1987, is actually quite unremarkable. Barnes is shown resplendent in his typically late-eighties skintight kit, seemingly controlling a ball which isn't even in the shot. In any other circumstance, it would have been dumped by the photographer as a nothing picture.

Yet this is no normal circumstance, for that picture has become one of the most symbolic sporting photographs ever taken, because of what can be seen in the bottom left-hand corner. It is a single banana and when you understand that Barnes wasn't controlling a ball, but was instead back-heeling that banana from the pitch, you will surely understand why it is so symbolic and what it has come to represent.

Ironically, Barnes never made much of it at the time and in numerous interviews since has highlighted the fact that bananas, monkey chants and especially verbal abuse had been the norm for years. Certainly, as someone who had followed both Barnes and his team-mate Luther Blissett around the country for years with Watford, I'd heard them take horrific stick at grounds such as the Den and Roker

Park, but in typically Watford fashion, we Watford fans had simply raised our game and given them even more support. The colour of their skin was never an issue with us, but it clearly was with others, because in many cases the vitriol directed at black players at the time wasn't simply designed to put them off their game, it was about something much deeper – hate and fear. The publication of this astonishing picture changed things overnight, for it finally made people consider the impact of racist abuse from the perspective of those on the receiving end, not as players, but as individuals. For the vast majority, it did not make for a comfortable experience.

The real tragedy, of course, is not that it had taken over a hundred years of black players' involvement in our national game for this change to begin, it's that by the time that the folly of racism was finally recognised, hundreds of individuals had been forced, through no fault of their own, to endure the type of sustained hatred that only those who have experienced it can comprehend. The fact that most of them rose above it speaks volumes about their dignity, pride and courage, but, equally, it says everything about those who let it happen. And we should be under no illusions here. As we shall see, some of the things that went on were beyond shameful. The history of black players within our national sport is not entirely something of which anyone should be proud.

However, it seems that things started very differently, because while until recently it was widely believed that the first black player in Britain was a gentleman called Arthur Wharton, who signed for Rotherham United in 1889, this is not actually the case. When looking through a variety of old programmes and documents relating to the early Scottish game, researchers became curious as to the identity of a Queens Park player from the 1870s, who had what they somewhat bizarrely referred to as 'an adolescent face and distinctive features'.

Further digging eventually revealed his identity to be Andrew Watson. The son of a wealthy Scotsman, he was born in British Guiana in 1857 and returned to Britain to study first at Rugby, then at Glasgow University. While studying in Glasgow Watson developed a love of football and such was his talent that he was signed by Maxwell FC in 1874, thus making him the first black player to play the game in

Britain. However, within five years his skill had attracted the attention of the country's most prestigious club, Queens Park, and Watson signed for them in 1879, eventually being a part of the 1882 Scottish Cup final-winning side and earning the accolade of being the first black player to feature in a British cup-winning team.

Such was Watson's talent that he even won three caps for Scotland and actually captained the team which beat England 6–1 at the Kennington Oval in 1881. This makes him not only the first black to play international football in Britain, but also the first non-white to captain his country. As if that wasn't enough, between 1883 and 1885 Watson also earned the honour of being the first black player in England when he played for London Swifts.

When he eventually retired from playing, this incredible man returned to Queens Park, where he became club secretary, thus becoming the first black to hold power in a British football club's boardroom. By any standards, Watson had an amazing career, but when you consider that he was a black immigrant in a sport where non-whites were unheard of and in a city like Glasgow where outsiders were hardly welcomed with open arms, it is simply stunning.

There is still much research to be done into the life and times of Andrew Watson, but his existence has undoubtedly had a huge impact on the history of black players within our game, primarily because, if he did encounter racism, it didn't appear to impact on his career either as a player or as an administrator – something which sadly cannot be said for the late, great Arthur Wharton.

Wharton was born in what is now Ghana in 1865 and was the son of mixed-race parents. His mother was actually a member of the Ghanaian royal family, while his father was half-Scottish, half-Grenadian. In 1886, Wharton came to England to train as a missionary in Staffordshire. However, boredom with the world of academia and religious life led him to leave school to forge a career based on his undoubted sporting talents. Initially, this meant athletics where, in July 1886, he set a new world record for the hundred yards dash. This soon brought him to the attention of a variety of football clubs and later that same year he signed as a semi-professional player for Preston North End, before turning fully professional in 1889 with Rotherham United.

As a goalkeeper at a time when attacking players could legitimately shoulder-charge the man between the sticks as they went for goal, Wharton rapidly developed some unique defences to shield himself from injury, the most famous being a trick of grabbing hold of the crossbar and hauling himself out of the way while swinging his legs wildly to kick the ball away. It was also not unknown for him to catch the ball between his legs or even to get his revenge in first!

In 1894, Wharton was poached by Sheffield United as their main keeper, part of the deal being the opportunity to take over the Sportsman Cottage pub in Button Lane. Sadly, the move wasn't a success, not simply because age was catching up on him and there was a new and younger keeper called Bill 'Fatty' Foulke pushing for his place, but because by this time Wharton's fondness for alcohol had begun to take hold.

When Foulke eventually took over between the sticks, Arthur left United and drifted from club to club, before eventually retiring from the game in 1902. Tragically, Arthur Wharton died in 1930 a penniless alcoholic and spent sixty-seven years in an unmarked grave in Edlington Cemetery near Doncaster, forgotten by the game he had served with such distinction.

For many, the story of this amazing man is a reflection of the racist attitudes that existed in the game both then and, to a certain extent, to this day. However, that is a distortion of the truth for Wharton was no victim. Indeed, in many respects, despite his wealthy background and the colour of his skin, he became a genuine northern working-class hero who was known for fighting back against those who abused him. That is not to deny the suffering he must have endured, though, because that was clearly all too real. While at Preston, for example, his name was mentioned as a possible England keeper, but due to the prejudices of the time, he was never selected. One can only imagine how that must have felt.

Thankfully, there is now a stone on the grave of Arthur Wharton and his memory has been brought back into the public domain through a book about his life and numerous articles. There has even been a picture of him included in an exhibition of British sporting heroes at the National Portrait Gallery in London.

Yet without wishing to ignore the colour of his skin, racism is not the reason why he ended up where and how he did, and to claim that it is does him a disservice and undermines his many achievements. The demon drink ruined Wharton, just as it has thousands of others since. It is as simple as that.

However, while Watson and Wharton made unique and vital contributions to the history of Britain's black footballers, they are not, in many people's opinion, including mine, the most important figures of their time. That honour is held by the third of this esteemed list, Walter Tull, a man for whom adversity seems to have become not simply a way of life, but a challenge which he beat at every opportunity.

Tull's father came to Britain from Barbados in 1876. The son of a slave, he lived in Folkestone, married a local girl and they had six children. When Walter was just seven, his mother died and two years later so did his father, leaving the six children alone. Sadly, their stepmother was unable to care for all six and arranged for Walter and his brother Edward to be placed in the care of the local Methodist church. Both eventually ended up in an orphanage in Bethnal Green, East London.

Incredibly, despite the tough environment, both boys grew into fine young men. Edward was eventually adopted by a Scottish family and became a successful dentist, while Walter began playing football for Clapton FC. He won medals in the FA Amateur Cup, London County Amateur Cup and London Senior Cup, and exhibited sufficient skill that in 1909 the *Football Star* called him 'the catch of the season' and the *Daily Chronicle* described him as having 'a class superior to that shown by most of his colleagues'.

Later that year, Walter signed as a professional for Tottenham Hotspur, but in a game against Bristol City he experienced his first taste of racist abuse. The reaction was incredible. Both clubs were outraged by the incident and the press went crazy. One reporter even went so far as to go into print and say, 'Let me tell those Bristol hooligans that Tull is so clean in mind and method as to be a model for all white men who play football whether they be amateur or professional. In point of ability, if not actual achievement, Tull was the best forward on the field.'

But for Tull the experience was a traumatic one. So badly did it affect him that he played only a handful of games for Tottenham and in 1911 was sold to Northampton Town for what was quoted at the time as being 'a heavy transfer fee'. There, Tull was revitalised. He became their biggest star and played 110 games for them as a wing-half, but in 1914, just as he was on the verge of a transfer to the mighty Glasgow Rangers, war broke out. Like many of his generation, Walter Tull immediately enlisted in the Army and joined the Seventeenth (First Football) Battalion of the Middlesex Regiment – a battalion made up almost entirely of professional footballers!

There were, however, no special privileges and in spite of their skill on the football field, the battalion was soon in the front line, where Tull excelled as a leader. So much so, that he soon attained the rank of sergeant. At the end of 1916, having endured the horrors of the first battle of the Somme, Tull was invalided home suffering from trench foot, but his bravery had so impressed his senior officers that he was recommended for officer training and when he was fully recovered was sent to cadet training school at Gailes in Scotland.

It is impossible to overstate the significance of this for at that time military law actually excluded any Negro or person of colour from holding any kind of command as officers. Yet thanks to the persistence of his superiors, in May 1917 Tull took the King's commission and became the first black officer in the British Army.

Upon graduation, Second Lieutenant Tull was sent to the Italian front as an officer in the Twenty-third (Second Football) Battalion of the Middlesex Regiment. He received a mention in dispatches for an assault on the enemy during the first battle of Piave and in doing so became the first black British officer to lead white troops into battle, before he and his men returned to France, where they fought in the second battle of the Somme.

Tragically, on 25 March 1918, Second Lieutenant Walter Tull was killed while leading an assault on enemy troops near the village of Favreuil. He was just twenty-nine years old. Such was his popularity among his men that many tried to rescue him, despite heavy German machine gun fire, but their efforts were in vain as Tull had died almost immediately from a single gunshot wound. He was posthumously awarded the British War and Victory Medal and recommended for a Military Cross for his part in the assault.

It is to this amazing man's credit that at a time when the class divide was still the backbone of the Empire, his commanding officer broke the news to his brother Edward personally. Indeed, records show that he remarked, 'The battalion and company have lost a faithful officer, and personally I have lost a friend.'

Yet sadly, even though obituaries labelled him as being 'every inch an officer and a gentleman' his death soon faded from the public consciousness. The death of a black, working-class orphan was seemingly not considered worthy of any kind of permanent record. To an extent, this is understandable, especially given the fact that Tull was just one individual in a generation decimated by the Great War, but it is a shame. While both Andrew Watson and Arthur Wharton were outstanding men and important figures in the history of British football, Walter Tull was a true British hero who would and should have been an inspirational figure for all those who followed in his wake. The fact that racial discrimination continued to infect both football and the military until fairly recently is a dreadful slur on a great man's ultimate sacrifice.

Despite the loss of so many men on the field of battle, the game in post-war Britain soon returned to normal with a small but significant number of black players being signed by clubs. The most notable of these was Jack Leslie, a London-born, Anglo-African who scored more than 400 goals for Plymouth between 1921 and 1935.

Inevitably, like most players at that time, Leslie suffered racist abuse on a regular basis, yet his skill as both a player and a goal-scorer left many supporters in no doubt that he was one of the great players of his era. They were right and, eventually, Jack Leslie was informed by his manager that he had been selected to play for England.

However, the official notification never arrived and for the rest of his life Leslie was convinced that this was because someone at the FA had realised he was black. While no official proof remains, his theory was almost certainly correct, marking this down as one of the most shameful episodes in the history of the game in this country.

At this point, we need to take a leap forward, because while players such as John Parris (who played for Northampton Town in the thirties and forties, and was the first non-white to play for Wales), Jamaican-born Lloyd Delapenha (who scored ninety goals in 260 appearances for Middlesbrough between 1950–57), Giles Heron (the first black player to appear for Celtic in 1951) and the many other black and Asian players who ran out for clubs in the intervening years were important in their own way, the next individual we should look at was the most famous black player of the sixties, Albert Johanneson.

What marks Johanneson out as significant is not his 197 appearances for Leeds United nor the fact that he was the first black player to appear in an FA Cup final, it's that as one of the few black players to appear in the upper echelons of the English game at that time, the racist abuse he was forced to endure was so overt and horrific. Even worse, it was compounded by the fact that it came from both fans and opposing players, but was often dismissed as nothing more than simple name-calling. Like many of his contemporaries, Johanneson was often shaken by the vitriol aimed at him, but the sheer scale of it inevitably had a debilitating effect, both on the man and his performances. As a result, he developed a reputation for suffering from 'stage fright' and after retiring from the game drifted into obscurity. Tragically, he died in 1995, aged just fifty-three years. A victim of depression and alcoholism, he was found alone in an empty Leeds high-rise flat and was so broke a single seashell was listed among his few possessions. It was a sad and undignified end for a great player.

Clearly, Johanneson suffered from the continued existence of racial myths that had dogged the careers of black players in Britain for years. Indeed, in many minds his frequent losses of confidence actually enforced those myths, for they lent credence to the theories that black players had no stomach for a fight, that they couldn't play in the cold weather and even that Africans couldn't play in boots! But as the seventies approached, the arrival of increasing numbers of African and West Indian immigrants meant that everything was about to change.

By the late sixties, the first generation of black Britons were already well established and in a sporting context individuals had enjoyed success in boxing and athletics, as well as football. Yet for many black youths at that time, role models would have been either white footballers or players such as Pele, who had already gained a reputation as the world's greatest player and who, thanks to TV coverage, had been able to show his skills to an eager audience. But what they desperately needed was a black role model within the English game and in 1969 he finally arrived in the shape of an unassuming striker from Bermuda called Clyde Best.

That Best played for West Ham is no accident. The club had always drawn talent from the local community and already had a number of black youths on their books, but the key to Best's success was TV. Programmes such as *The Big Match* took him into homes the length and breadth of the country and as one of only a handful of black players turning out regularly in the First Division at that time, he could not help but stand out. For the first time Britain's black youth had a player they could relate to and who provided proof that there was certainly room for them within the upper echelons of the national game.

Yet truth be told, Best never achieved the heights of team-mates such as Bobby Moore or Geoff Hurst. Many believe that part of the reason for this was because, week in and week out, he was subjected to a stream of barracking and criticism, not just from the crowd, but often from the media, who labelled him lazy. Writing in 1983, Brian Woolnough even claimed that, 'He is perhaps the best example of why it has taken so long for managers, coaches and the public to accept the coloured stars. Best would be brilliant one game, bad the next, and the question marks against the black players' stamina, power and determination hung over them for years.'

But Best had opened the floodgates and by the end of the seventies there were over fifty young black players playing regularly in England, many of whom were home-grown. These included such famous names as Viv Anderson, who not only won numerous domestic and European honours with Nottingham Forest, but became the first black player to be capped by England, and West Brom's famous 'Three Degrees' – Cyrille Regis, Brendon Batson and Laurie Cunningham.

However, in spite of this, the spectre of racism remained and actually grew in the seventies, as right-wing groups such as the National Front made serious inroads into the increasing numbers of hooligan groups. Newspapers such as the *Bulldog*, which often and openly incited hatred against black players, were on open sale outside grounds, while club badges, flags and scarves were often doctored to include right-wing symbols or slogans. Similarly, the throwing of bananas and fruit, as well as the chanting of monkey noises, were all directed at black players, in many cases even those on the fans' own team!

Now to some reading this over twenty-five years later it is hard to imagine what it was like back then. After all, these days, when even lone racist voices are rare inside grounds, the idea that an entire end could indulge in such vile abuse beggars belief. Yet at many grounds such behaviour was the norm in the seventies and eighties and so, in an effort to both educate those who know no better and remind those who were there just how bad things really were back then, it is right that we provide a brief example. I can think of nothing which does that better than Selhurst Park in 1982 and the visit of Chelsea.

The game itself was on the Easter Monday of a season in which both clubs resided in the Second Division. Chelsea, already known for having a huge hooligan following and an extremely racist element among its support, had all but taken over the ground and had spent the first half racially abusing the great Vince Hilaire. A short time into the second half, the Chelsea bench decided to make a change and up to the line stepped Paul Canonville. A gifted young striker, the club had high hopes for him, but the fans had other ideas. Canonville would not only be making his first-team debut, he was also about to become the first black player to turn out for Chelsea. However, the reaction to his appearance on the line has been described as horrific.

Almost immediately, the Chelsea support began hurling abuse at him, and this wasn't simple monkey chants, but Nazi salutes and songs such as 'We don't need the nigger, we don't need the nigger, la, la, la, la'. Now this didn't just come from a small group, but almost the entire Chelsea support, which, remember, was situated in all four corners of the ground. Not only that, but it continued for the first ten to fifteen minutes that he was on the pitch – and it was all directed at one of their own players. Shameful enough, but, sadly, Paul Canonville's experience of racism from Chelsea fans was far from over. Over the next season it became so bad that a certain section of the Chelsea support even put together a league table excluding Canonville's goals.

For Canonville, as for other black players at the time, the fear such behaviour must have generated is beyond comprehension. Yet slowly, their tenacity began to pay off, especially at clubs such as West Brom, where the fans soon came to realise that the Three Degrees were a huge asset to the club, and at Watford where both Luther Blissett and John Barnes had driven the club to previously unimagined heights under the stewardship of Graham Taylor.

Equally, the success of black players, especially at inner city clubs with large local immigrant populations, began to draw black supporters into grounds, albeit in small numbers. And as more and more black players made the breakthrough, the domestic game finally began to see a decline in racism on the terraces, not as a result of any pressure from the FA, the government or even the clubs, but because fans began to realise the stupidity of abusing black players on opposing teams while cheering on those who played for them.

However, although locally things were beginning to change, at international level it was still occasionally very ugly. Prior to his debut for England in 1982, Cyrille Regis received a bullet through the post with a warning that he would receive another one should he dare to step out on to the hallowed Wembley turf. Undeterred, Regis went on to score on his debut, but was actually booed by a section of the home support even as he celebrated the goal. And in 1984, John Barnes was singled out for abuse by England fans during a tour of South America. This despite his goal against Brazil, which is still regarded as one of the greatest ever.

Thankfully, such incidents became increasingly rare as the eighties drew to a close, a development due in no small part to the increasing number of black players within the game and the fact that some had featured in a series of big-money transfers, most notably Paul Ince from West Ham to Manchester United and John Barnes from Watford to Liverpool. Indeed, Barnes' move to Anfield in 1987 is significant in many ways, not least because the city had developed a reputation for being resistant towards black players and the arrival of one of the biggest names in English football helped dispel that rumour once and for all, at least in the red half of the city.

Tragically, within two years of Barnes' arrival, Liverpool were to feature in an event which not only changed the face of English football forever, but had a significant impact on the growing anti-racism movement – Hillsborough.

The death of ninety-six Liverpool fans on 15 April 1989 and the subsequent Lord Justice Taylor report forced the game to take a long, hard look at what it had become. The result was the formation of the Premiership and a whole new type of footballing experience. However, it is fair to say that, not for the first time, it was commercial considerations that were ultimately responsible for this change. The role of supporters, not to mention the impact on them, merited barely a passing thought among those who saw a way of making millions.

The exception to this was Lord Justice Taylor's recommendation that new laws be introduced to deal with a variety of problems, including racist abuse. It was a recommendation the Government was quick to latch on to and the 1991 Football Offences Act made racist chanting at football matches unlawful. Sadly, it turned out to be a fairly useless piece of legislation, as it defined chanting as the 'repeated uttering of any words or sounds in concert with one or more others'. As a result, individuals could only be charged under the 1986 Public Order Act for using foul language, a loophole that allowed numerous offenders to escape conviction.

It was still a significant step, because it recognised and acknowledged the lingering problem of racism among a small minority of fans and, as a result, gained widespread support, but what was needed was something that would involve the fans and provide a way of helping them spread the anti-racism message. In 1993, it arrived when the Campaign for Racial Equality (CRE) and the Professional Footballers' Association (PFA) launched Let's Kick Racism Out of Football (Kick Racism).

There had been numerous supporter-led initiatives before, most notably at Leeds United, a club with a history of right-wing involvement on its terraces, yet while Leeds Fans United Against Racism And Fascism enjoyed huge success in raising the profile of the problem and driving the far right out of Elland Road, like similar fan- and fanzine-led initiatives, it suffered from the age-old problem of being localised, whereas Kick Racism was established with the aim of involving everybody. It was an immediate success.

The strength of Kick Racism was that it had both a strategy and an awareness of the potential power it had at its disposal. By initially focussing on the professional game and providing each of the ninety-two clubs with a unique plan of action to combat racist abuse and encourage a positive approach to ethnic minorities among both their support and the local communities, they left the clubs with no option but to join in. To be fair, the majority were delighted to come on board, but there were those who remained sceptical. Some claimed that the campaign was highlighting a problem that was already in decline, while others made it clear that racism had never been a problem in their ground anyway, so why bother?

However, by the start of the 1994–95 season, ninety-one clubs had signed up and, more crucially, the anti-racism message had reached the fans who, in the main, embraced it with open arms. On the opening day of that season, *Kick It!*, a magazine funded by the Football Trust, was produced and distributed, together with 110,000 copies of a fanzine called *United Colours of Football*, which was given out free at grounds across the country. But key to the campaign was a ten-point plan to help the clubs combat racism both inside and outside grounds. This covered everything from making PA announcements and the removal of graffiti to taking disciplinary action against any player or member of staff who used racist abuse. Ironically, within a few months the latter was to play a significant role in an incident that rocked the game to its very core.

On 25 January 1995, Manchester United star Eric Cantona was sent off at Selhurst Park for an off-the-ball assault on Crystal Palace defender Richard Shaw. Suitably enraged, as he left the pitch Cantona reacted angrily to abuse from the crowd and launched what can only be described as a drop-kick at Palace fan Matthew Simmons.

It was an extraordinary and just about unprecedented incident, one which sent the papers into a frenzy with the majority calling for the Frenchman to be banned from the game forever if not jailed for assault. Yet almost immediately Cantona's legal team issued the claim that, while there could be no justification for his actions, they were in part understandable because he had been subjected to racist abuse. It was a claim that almost certainly saved Cantona from jail, but, more importantly, it was seized upon by the anti-racism movement for the simple reason that Eric Cantona was white – a fact made all the more relevant when allegations began to surface that Simmons had a murky political past.

John Barnes is famously quoted as saying, 'It took a white Frenchman to be assaulted in our league before racism was really taken seriously,' and while many would argue with that, there can be little doubt that, for the anti-racism campaigners, the Cantona incident was a cataclysmic event as it highlighted the fact that racism isn't always about black and white. Similarly, it forced the game and the authorities to acknowledge that many of the points raised by Kick Racism, in particular those relating to how stewards and the police deal with racism inside grounds, were valid. As a result, any idea of clubs simply paying lip service to the campaign were banished overnight.

However, there were plenty of people with whom events were not sitting comfortably. Many believed that Manchester United had ignored the potential implications and had selfishly played the race card with the sole aim of keeping Cantona's punishment as light as possible. Others questioned the idea that calling a Frenchman 'French' could, or indeed should, actually be considered racist in the same sense as the use of the work 'black'.

The problem was, in a country governed by a Labour Party obsessed with political correctness, the idea of anyone actually questioning anything relating to the problem of racism was almost unheard of and the few who actually dared were often subjected to accusations that they were themselves racist. So fearful of that label had people become that they were actually falling over themselves to make ever more outrageous statements in support of the Frenchman. For example, Sir Trevor Brooking, a man regarded as one of the few true gentlemen in the game, described it as 'the most horrendous incident involving a player I have ever witnessed at an English football ground', while the FA declared that, 'Such an incident brings shame on those involved as well as, more importantly, on the game itself.'

For many rank-and-file fans, enough was enough. Increasing numbers were becoming tired of being tarred with a particular brush and were unhappy at the portrayal of Cantona as some kind of anti-racist icon, when in reality he was nothing more than a thug who had assaulted a football fan for doing what the vast majority of fans have always accepted as their right – hurling abuse at opposing players. In addition, some were even beginning to question the continued need for an anti-racism movement at all. Black players had become an accepted and valued part of the game and, while there were still isolated incidents inside grounds, the game had been more successful in the fight against racism than just about any other area of British society.

However, just a few short weeks after the Cantona incident and before any serious debate could begin, the image of the game was dealt a crippling blow when rioting England fans forced the abandonment of a game against the Republic of Ireland in Dublin.

That a small number of far-right extremists were to blame for this incident is beyond question. At the time, many Britons were extremely unhappy at the fact that the Government had seemingly given in to Republican terrorism and the chant 'No surrender to the IRA' had been a sad feature of the travelling support for years. As a result, the opportunity for organisations such as the British National Party (BNP) and Combat 18 to travel to Ireland and make a political statement was simply too good to miss, and they succeeded beyond their wildest dreams. Suddenly, the issue of right-wing extremism and football was back on the front pages and despite the fact that the riot had far more to do with xenophobia than racism, any notion of questioning the need for an anti-racism movement had vanished, at least for the time being.

Later that year, spurred on by events at Selhurst Park and in Dublin, the FA gave the anti-racism campaigners a major fillip when they committed to the cause and established the Advisory Group Against Racism and Intimidation. With just about every aspect of the game now involved, from the governing bodies right through to the fans, Kick Racism was able to expand things even further by working more directly with the clubs and involving players in high-profile campaigns. Once again it proved a huge success, yet as the season passed just about everyone in the country was mindful of the fact that, potentially, it could all unravel very quickly for one specific reason – Euro 96. After all, if a small number of right-wing extremists could cause such disruption in Dublin, what might they be able to do in their home land?

In the event, they did nothing and neither did the hooligans, although, to be fair, the warnings of large-scale disorder had been largely whipped up by the police and the media, albeit for different reasons. Instead, the summer of 1996 will be remembered as a positive time for both the game and the country. Not only did England finally rediscover its love of our national game, but almost the entire population became caught up in the euphoria and, amazingly, the nation rediscovered some pride in itself. As a result, the Cross of St George, for so long tainted by the right wing, was won back and became an acceptable symbol of the national side's support.

Now, at last, the mood surrounding the game was one of genuine and real optimism. The Premier League was booming, thanks in no small part to the influx of foreign players, hooliganism had apparently been banished from football and the spectre of racism was on the wane as more and more supporters from ethnic minority groups began following the game. Buoyed by this, the following season Kick Racism finally took the battle into the grass roots of the game, through the launch of Kick It Out, an independent body funded by the FA, the PFA, the Football Trust and the Premier League.

Tasked with working with local groups and the regional football associations, Kick It Out's remit was to encourage more involvement with local ethnic communities and to work with young people to promote the anti-racism message. Once again, it enjoyed huge success, yet there was a dark cloud on the horizon.

In 1996, the Government had set up a football task force led by the former minister David Mellor MP. Mellor, who had been largely discredited as a football fan due to the revelation that he had changed his supporting allegiance from Fulham to Chelsea, was charged with putting together a report that would tackle a variety of issues affecting the game, ranging from players' wages right through to ticket prices and merchandising. Crucially, the task force also looked at the issue of racism and in 1997 it delivered its final report. It made for interesting, but uncomfortable, reading.

To be fair, many of the points it raised were valid in so much as there was, and remains, a need to encourage black and Asian fans into grounds and on to boards, yet it was the way it was delivered that caused the problem. It was quite simply forty-six pages of politically correct bullshit.

Not only did it suggest such things as having anti-racism statements included in everything from players' contracts to letting agreements for Sunday league pitches, it actually advocated the use of positive discrimination by suggesting that clubs be forced to send scouts to tournaments involving Asian amateur clubs and making it a condition of Football Trust funding that clubs implemented Kick It Out initiatives.

While the reaction to the report from the clubs and the authorities was one of typically warm acceptance, among many rank-and-file fans it didn't quite receive such a great reception. By now, increasing numbers were becoming irritated that the game they loved was being subjected to constant attack for being a hotbed of racism, when in reality that wasn't the case at all. Indeed, within the professional game in England the campaigns had been so successful that by the mid-nineties racist abuse and chanting had been all but eradicated from grounds, proof that the game had led the way in the battle against racism in Britain and that the foot soldiers in that fight had been the fans themselves, the vast majority of whom were white Anglo-Saxons. However, in Mellor's report, what little recognition there was for their efforts was more than offset by the attacks on the game and its failure to bring through an Asian player or manager. As a result, questions finally began to be asked in the pubs and on the terraces about the validity of those attacks and, equally, the motives of those who were making them.

The problem was that that is where they stayed, because not only did no one really know who to put those questions to, but, more importantly, there was also an understandable reluctance to go public and actually ask them. After all, in a nation already dominated by politically correct thinking, the fear of being labelled racist was – and remains – a very real one. It's a very easy label to throw at someone and it's a very difficult label to defend yourself against, as I know to my cost.

When Eddy and I discussed this very issue in both *Everywhere We Go* and *England, My England*, we received an amazing and universally supportive reaction to our thoughts on racism, patriotism and nationalism. Ironically, both books were full of praise for the work done by the anti-racism organisations at football and actually urged them to build on their success by taking the battle one step further and involving the anti-hooligan groups in their fight. Yet within months we had been tagged as extreme right-wingers for daring to put those thoughts in print and had even been targeted by one of the anti-Nazi organisations. It was all bollocks, of course, but while we were both prepared and able to deal with it, it proved conclusively that for anyone in the public eye, risking their career by asking pertinent questions of a campaign such as Kick Racism was unthinkable.

Similarly, the media organisations always tended to avoid anything controversial or negative relating to the anti-racism organisations for fear that it would backfire on them. While understandable to a degree, I have to say that I always regarded that as both cowardly and dangerous, primarily because it afforded people the power to manipulate situations to their advantage. Sadly, that was a power too many individuals were happy to abuse for one reason and one reason only.

That the drive to rid the grounds of racist behaviour had been an incredible success by the mid-nineties is beyond question, but in certain circles there is little doubt in my mind that this was probably being perceived as something of a disaster. For while no one was in any doubt that there remained a massive amount of work to be done outside the professional game, the top flight was where the publicity lay and publicity means funding. In effect, the top flight had been driving football's anti-racism gravy train and all those who had jumped on board were desperate to keep it running. If that meant hyping up the odd rare lapse inside a ground or manipulating situations to include a football-related racist element, even if no such element existed, then that is what they would do, aided in no small part by the fact that they would never be questioned or held to account for their actions. If anyone doubts that as the truth, then they need look no further than the aftermath of the tragic murder of black teenager Stephen Lawrence, who was stabbed to death on 22 April 1993 as he waited for a bus in Eltham's Well Hall Road.

The fact that Lawrence was the victim of a racist attack is beyond question and, quite rightly, his death sent shockwaves around the country. For obvious reasons I will not go into too much detail here, but suffice to say that the police fairly quickly arrested a number of white youths, all of whom were local. Eventually, due to lack of evidence, they were all released, but in many people's eyes they remain the only suspects for what remains an unsolved murder.

However, while the death of Stephen Lawrence opened up numerous debates surrounding the issue of racism in Britain and led to the now famous MacPherson report into the Metropolitan police, within the world of football it had a slightly less welcome impact. That's because the revelation (*sic*) that the suspects were supposedly football fans led to inferences that the clubs they followed had actually tolerated their racist behaviour on the terraces. Not for the first time, the club that suffered most from those inferences was Millwall.

To an already hostile press, 'violence', 'racism' and 'Millwall' had long been three words that went hand in hand, and so the arrests played into the papers' hands. It mattered not an iota that not one of the suspects supported the club or that Millwall, led by its chairmen Reg Burr and then the charismatic Theo Paphitis, had been among the most vociferous, not to mention successful, anti-racism campaigners within the game. It didn't even matter that Millwall isn't even the closest club to Eltham. What mattered was its firmly established reputation as the archetypal hooligan club and the reputation of the area as being a hotbed of right-wing activity, the latter being reinforced by the election of a BNP councillor in Millwall less than six months after the murder of Stephen Lawrence.

Ignoring the simple truth that the New Den isn't even in Millwall, the press were soon all over the club like a rash. Stories of racist chanting were apparently heard by undercover journalists and reports that BNP literature was being distributed outside the New Den on matchdays filled everything from the *Sun* to the *Guardian*. The attacks continued until the spring of 1999, but while everything was vehemently denied by the club and the long-suffering fans, the silence from both Kick Racism and the FA was damning. As a result, the mud was left well and truly stuck and the demonisation of Millwall and its supporters was all but complete. To its eternal credit, and despite being left high and dry with its 'reputation' ready to be trotted out at every opportunity, the club got on with the job of working with local ethnic community groups and enforcing some of the strictest anti-racism rules of any football club in Europe, but the damage had been done and, largely thanks to the whipping boy that is Millwall, racism had returned to football's agenda and would remain there for the foreseeable future. While this was the worst possible news for the game, at least the gravy train was firmly back on track.

CHAPTER NINE
THE PRESENT DAY

In almost every respect the nineties was one of the most significant decades in the history of the English game. The formation of the Premier League and the arrival of both all-seater stadia and BSkyB changed the game and the way we watch it forever. Equally, as a result of CCTV and intelligence-led policing, hooliganism had been all but banished from inside grounds and the number of racist incidents had tailed off to the extent that, on the rare occasions when they did happen, they were big news.

While much of the credit for that must go to the CRE and the various anti-racism initiatives targeted at football, it was also due in no small part to the ever-growing and extremely positive impact being made by black players on the English game. It has been estimated that of the 2000 professional players in England during the 1999–2000 season, over 300 were black, with a large percentage of those being British. This was certainly reflected in the national side, with players such as Paul Ince and Sol Campbell having firmly established themselves in the first team.

It is also fair to say that the 1991 Football Offences Act had been a major factor in the battle to drive racists out of grounds, but it had one major flaw. Subsection 2(a) defined the act of chanting as 'the repeated uttering of any words or sounds in concert with one or more others'. What this meant in real terms was that seeking a conviction against an individual indulging in racist chanting or abuse was extremely difficult.

However, in 1999, that loophole was finally closed and the police and the game were handed the weapon they had wanted. With Euro 2000 fast approaching, security concerns high on the agenda and the MacPherson report alleging institutionalised racism in the force still ringing firmly in their ears, it was a weapon the police were very public about intending to use.

They had every reason to be concerned. During the 1998 World Cup, Marseille had witnessed scenes of major disorder which seemed to not simply support but enhance the reputation of England fans as being the worst in Europe. As a result, the national side had faced the very real possibility of expulsion from the tournament and with the media full of images of shaven-headed males being frog-marched into captivity by French riot police against a backdrop of English flags, there were renewed allegations of widespread xenophobia among the English support.

Yet while xenophobia is just as unpalatable as racism – hate is hate, after all, be it for another nation or another race – in many ways it is also very different and a number of commentators gave voice to the idea that there may well have been more to events in Marseille than met the eye. Some claimed it was an attempt by the right wing to build on the perceived success of Dublin three years earlier, while others claimed that it was a reaction to years of oppression of English patriotism. Others, myself included, preferred to believe that it was a combination of both, fired up by aggression from the locals and the French police.

However, whatever the rights or wrongs, all parties were agreed that Euro 2000 had the potential for real problems, but even as everyone was gearing up for the summer, things began to look bleak. In the January, two Leeds United players, Lee Bowyer and Jonathan Woodgate, were charged with involvement in an assault on Asian student Sarfraz Najeib. Not surprisingly, the papers went to town and when allegations surfaced that just prior to the attack someone had supposedly been heard to shout 'do you want some, Paki?' there were calls for the pair to be charged with racially aggravated assault.

However, the CPS soon realised that even if it could be proven that one of the group had indeed shouted this out, it would certainly have been impossible to prove which one. So sure in the knowledge that a charge of racially aggravated assault would never stand up in court and well aware of the potential implications, both legal and political, of going after a charge it knew would never stick, the CPS reluctantly decided to lower its sights and go for a lesser charge; one on which it knew there was at least a sporting chance of securing a conviction.

In spite of the fact that the decision was correct and would at least result in a court case, the anti-racism lobby was outraged. Even the announcement that the two players would not be considered for selection for the England squad until the case had been through the legal process failed to appease them. They wanted Woodgate and Bowyer hung out to dry as confirmation that the game was riddled with racism.

However, even as the furore surrounding Bowyer and Woodgate raged, in the March England striker Emile Heskey was forced to endure horrific racial abuse from both Yugoslavian supporters and players during the under twenty-one Euro 2000 play-off in Barcelona.

Once again, the issue of racism and football was thrust back to the fore, only this time it was different. This racism wasn't *by* anyone English, it was against one of our leading players. Quite rightly, the FA and Kick it Out were incensed and made immediate complaints to UEFA who, already concerned about the increasing racism involving sides from Eastern Europe, issued a stern warning to the Yugoslav FA. However, yet again it failed to take anything approaching action by way of punishment. Even the English media were furious at what they regarded as a terrible display of double standards, yet even as the arguments continued the game was overtaken by a tragedy – the murders of Chris Loftus and Kevin Speight in Istanbul on 5 April 2000.

It had long been known that violence involving Turkish football fans was a major problem and English football supporters had suffered directly from it on more than one occasion. Yet just like Italy, Holland and Germany, Turkey had always seemingly escaped any kind of sanction, while even the merest sniff of trouble involving the English game had attracted the full wrath of Sepp Blatter.

Now, ironically, those same fans looked towards FIFA and UEFA for action, but, tragically, yet again none was forthcoming. To make matters worse, not only did Galatasaray go on to beat Arsenal in the UEFA Cup final that year, but when trouble erupted in the centre of

Copenhagen, the English fans were heavily criticised by all parties for their role in the violence, even though most reports accused local Turks of starting it.

To say that there was a real sense of injustice among the nation's football supporters was an understatement. While the English game had done more than any other to deal with the combined problems of hooliganism and racism, it was clear that in many eyes we were still perceived as being the problem. As a result, more and more people began to believe that the failure to punish both Yugoslavia and Turkey, coupled with the continued criticism of our game and its fans, had more to do with attacking England and the English than it had with the security of global football.

It was a situation tailor-made for the xenophobes and with Turkish fans using the internet to voice all kinds of threats against the English travelling support, the nation headed for Euro 2000 expecting the worst. As we have seen elsewhere, largely as a result of some appalling policing at the hands of the Belgian authorities, it almost got it. However, one real positive was that fears of large-scale and coordinated attacks on both Turkish football fans and members of the local Turkish population, involving Belgian neo-Nazis as well as Dutch, German and English hooligans, proved unfounded. Indeed, aside from rumours that an organisation called the England Volunteer Group had been trying to stir up trouble in Belgium, there had been no evidence of any serious racist activity being perpetuated by, or involving any, England fans at the tournament.

Not surprisingly, the fallout from both Istanbul and Euro 2000 was immense, but one of the more interesting developments was that, almost for the first time, English football fans, black, white and Asian, began to look to Kick Racism, Kick it Out and even the CRE to ask not only what it was doing to protect players against the increasing tide of racism when overseas, but what it was doing to protect them. Racism is racism after all, no matter what the colour of the victim's skin. The answer, sadly, was very little. Indeed, in some quarters the sheer irony of white supporters complaining about anyone being subjected to racist abuse was almost a source of mirth.

To add insult to injury, March 2001 saw the release of the final report by the Government's Working Group into Football Disorder. Not only did this support many of the recommendations made by David Mellor's Task Force, it actually went further by advocating such things as compulsory cultural diversity training programmes for stewards. This, in spite of the admission that arrests for racist chanting inside grounds in England had declined to just thirty-five during the 1999–2000 season.

Chaired by Lord Bassam, the terms of reference for the report were, 'To reduce, by means other than new legislation, the level of football disorder associated with the supporters of the England team and English national and club sides playing overseas; and to that end, to consider measures both to prevent misbehaviour by existing supporters and to encourage the presence at such matches of a larger proportion of decent supporters who are opposed to football disorder and the attitudes which prompt it.' To be fair, many of the things it dealt with, particularly in relation to grass roots football, local ethnic communities and the image of the national side, were both admirable and long overdue. Furthermore, plans to scrap the England members' club and replace it with a new supporters' group, thus providing better control of ticket distribution as well as stricter vetting of all potential members, were widely welcomed, as was increased support for the fans' embassies at tournaments and recognition of the decline in trouble involving English clubs playing in Europe.

However, there were certain aspects that left a bad taste in the mouth, not least the very real sense that much of the content had been driven by political correctness. This idea appeared to be supported by the fact that, while it referred constantly to both racism and xenophobia, there was not a single mention of patriotism on any of the fifty-three pages that made up the report – strange, given that inclusion rather than exclusion had always, and quite rightly, been at the heart of the drive to deal with the racism issue.

To many people, this was more than a lost opportunity, it was actually a backward step. Indeed, one of the major complaints levelled at the report was the constant implication that hooliganism, racism and xenophobia are one and the same thing, which they patently are not. However, by linking them together the report once again clouded the idea of English patriotism as being both a positive and inclusive thing for the national game.

I have to say, as one of the individuals who participated in the working group, I have some sympathy with this viewpoint. I was actually present at a meeting where issues relating to the promotion of Englishness were discussed at length. One of these concerned the national anthem. My recollection is that the idea of a specifically English anthem, such as 'Jerusalem' or 'Land of Hope and Glory', would be a very positive step forward, yet there is no mention of it at all in the final draft. One can only speculate as to why.

Curiously, soon after the report was released, Lord Bassam was removed from the position and, in the fullness of time, many of the good ideas advocated in the report slipped away. But it was becoming clear that there was a growing sense of grievance among fans that not only were their efforts being undermined, but that the debate was all one way. There was still no one with the profile, power or will to stand up and counter some of the things being said and not only was the game suffering, but, by association, so were they. For the first time in years, the terrace grapevine began to show signs of a clear shift in attitudes and racism, long thought of on the terraces of England as being simply a black and white issue, began to take on a new form. The target for this new intolerance was the Asian community.

The reasons for this were many, varied and in some respects had little or nothing to do with football. The terraces have traditionally been one of the places where the average working man gives vent to his thoughts and opinions and the steady drip-drip-drip of political correctness that had resulted in the suppression of English history and patriotism had long been a source of both heated debate and resentment. Furthermore, with many grounds situated in the middle of large Asian communities, all too often many of the perceived problems relating to the concept of multiculturalism in terms of integration were laid bare. Little wonder that in the past the right wing had regarded many of those same grounds as vital in terms of recruitment.

Indeed, in April 2001 racism and politics clashed head on when a sizable group of Stoke City supporters attending a match in Oldham were blamed for inflaming racial tensions when they insisted on walking through multi-racial areas of the town on their way to and from the stadium. As a result, fighting broke out, which quickly grew into a series of major race riots.

In a purely football sense a major factor in the growing unrest was the continued obsession the various anti-racism organisations had with the game's failure to bring through an Asian player or attract legions of Asian fans through the terraces of grounds that were, in many instances, on their very doorstep. The fact that both of these apparent failures were routinely being used as sticks with which to beat the game, yet could and should have been countered with fairly obvious answers, simply reinforced the lack of balanced representation. Furthermore, the aftermath of the murders of the Leeds United fans in Istanbul and the apparent failure to secure any kind of justice for the two families continued to be a source of anger, particularly among the hooligan community. However, if things were simmering in the summer of 2001, they came to the boil in September that year, when Muslim terrorists flew airliners into the Twin Towers in New York.

In a nation already suspicious of the Islamic religion, news reports of groups of British citizens not only celebrating the attacks but advocating more, outraged the population. Despite the fact that the vast majority of British Muslims were equally outraged, anti-Islamic feeling spread through large sections of the nation and, even though much of it was as a result of ignorance, it found a warm welcome among certain groups on certain terraces.

This was, however, a different type of racism. In the past, abuse had usually been directed at individuals, be they players or fans, but now things had changed. Asian fans were rare, Asian players non-existent. As a result, at a number of clubs abuse took the form of taunts aimed at belittling the towns and cities of opposing clubs. The best examples were a resurgence of the old chant 'Town full of Pakis, you're just a town full of Pakis' and 'I'd rather be a Paki than a Turk'.

As 2001 moved towards its close, the acquittal of both Jonathan Woodgate and Lee Bowyer on charges relating to the assault on Sarfraz Najeib did little to ease growing tensions, and indications were that the game would see a rise in reported racist incidents for the first time in years. However, while the authorities were worried, their immediate priorities lay elsewhere, for England was heading to Japan and Korea for the 2002 World Cup.

To say that there were concerns about holding the tournament in the Far East would be an understatement. Not only was hooliganism a totally unknown quantity in the Far East, but the cultural differences and inherent possibilities for causing offence were immense. However, while even the most moronic of hooligans seemed to be able to grasp the idea that doing anything to upset authority in Korea was a seriously bad idea, the Japanese were a different matter. For obvious reasons, there were very real fears that we would see numerous incidents of xenophobic activity among a section of the English support. In the event, these fears proved totally unjustified. Indeed, the England fans returned from the tournament to universal and unparalleled praise for their behaviour. Sadly, this positive step was not replicated elsewhere.

In the September, racist abuse hurled at Arsenal's black players, most notably Thierry Henry, soured their 4–0 victory over Eindhoven in Holland. Then, just a few weeks later, England's trip to Bratislava for a 2004 World Cup qualifier against Slovakia was marred by some of the worst racist abuse anyone had seen or heard for years. Once again, the main target for the abuse was Emile Heskey, although Ashley Cole also received his fair share.

What marked this incident out as significant was not simply the abuse, it was the volume of it. At one stage, it seemed that, with the exception of the English support, the entire stadium was jeering the England players. Heskey was even subjected to monkey chants from a group of stretcher staff when he went to collect a ball for a throw-in!

To make matters worse, fighting broke out when the local riot police waded into a group of England fans in scenes reminiscent of Rome in 1997. Ironically, many claimed that the catalyst for the trouble was anger at the taunts aimed at the England players. However, the FA, mindful of the fact that only the night before two England fans had received gunshot wounds after a confrontation at a nightclub in the city, and wary of rumours that a group of right-wing England fans had been present in the ground, erred on the side of caution. It did however, register an immediate complaint with UEFA about the racist abuse and some of the crowd control measures employed by the Slovakian police.

For its part, the Slovakian FA issued an immediate apology and promised to write to both players personally, while UEFA, aware that it had only recently issued a fresh ten-point directive to combat racism, eventually hit the Slovak FA with a 60,000 Swiss franc fine. This was the second highest penalty ever handed out for racist behaviour.

While this sent a clear message to European football, racism continued to be an increasing problem at home. In the November, Manchester United striker Dwight Yorke was on the receiving end of the infamous monkey chants at Sunderland's Stadium of Light, while Leicester City's British-born Turkish star Muzzy Izzet was subjected to abuse from Leeds United fans at Filbert Street.

To make matters worse, in April 2003, with the invasion of Iraq still raging, the England versus Turkey Euro 2004 qualifier was marred by violence off the pitch and accusations of racist abuse by England fans aimed at Turkish players and supporters. However, although much of the inevitable and understandable criticism of the fans at the Stadium of Light revolved around the infamous 'I'd rather be a Paki than a Turk' chant that had echoed around the ground, this was more of a xenophobic than racist incident; its roots almost entirely grounded in Istanbul and the murder of the two Leeds United fans three years previously.

Inevitably, and quite rightly, UEFA was outraged and eventually hammered the FA with a £70,000 fine, but fears were increasingly being expressed about the qualifier away leg and It became clear that the FA was considering not taking up its allocation of tickets. Support for this idea came not only from sections of the press, but also from the police, who had genuine security concerns. In the event, the FA agreed. This decision not only left those fans who did make the journey – some of whom had not missed an England trip for over twenty years – to fend for themselves, it equally, for the first time, conceded defeat to the minority. Not that the FA saw it like that of course, its argument being that any trouble or xenophobia involving England fans in Turkey would almost certainly have resulted in the team being banned from Euro 2004.

Although a contentious decision, the FA's stance seemed to be endorsed by the release of two reports which appeared to indicate a sharp rise in racism among fans in England. The first claimed that forty-one per cent of supporters had seen or heard either racist abuse or chanting in the previous two years and an additional twenty-seven per cent had done so in the last five years. The second, the annual Home Office report into football-related arrests and banning orders, quoted a fifty-seven per cent increase in racist-related arrests at games in the 2002–03 season. However, as with all such things, if you're looking to back something up statistics can be made to say just about anything. For example, the Home Office report, as we have seen elsewhere, is traditionally used simply to justify the huge amount of money poured into policing the great game.

To be fair to the police, in their report they make it clear that the increase is almost entirely due to their lower tolerance levels of racist abuse. They also include the fact that the total number of racist-related arrests was seventy-four (up from forty-seven the previous year). Still seventy-four too many admittedly, but a small proportion of the 3695 arrests which made up the total figure for that season and a minuscule number compared to the 28 million who attended games in the top flight.

Yet in the media coverage of these reports information such as the actual number of arrests were more often than not curiously absent, as was any detail of just how many supporters were polled, where they came from or even what colour they were. Not that the guys at Kick it Out were concerned about simple trivia. Indeed, Piara Powar, the director of Kick It Out, inevitably welcomed the reports and said, 'Until arrest figures match the reality of the problem, fans and players will not have the confidence to make reports and black and Asian fans will continue to stay away.'

Yet these simple omissions and the subsequent attacks on the game – *The Times* went so far as to say that the problem of terrace racism was 'endemic' – not only painted an inaccurate picture of life on the terraces of England, but once again cast the game in a very negative light, inevitably undermining the progress made by the game in recent years.

Things were not helped when in the September poor Emile Heskey again came under a barrage of racist abuse from supporters in Eastern Europe when playing for England. This time the guilty nation was Macedonia. Immediately, and quite rightly, Trevor Phillips, head of the CRE, called for tougher action against teams whose supporters racially abused players. More importantly, he finally made a point that a number of supporters had been making when he said that the abuse and assault suffered by black players was now such that it had begun to constitute unfair interference in the game.

However, while Phillips urged UEFA and FIFA to go along the points-docking or even expulsion route, Liverpool boss Gerard Houllier went even further when he let it be known that he was prepared to risk the sack by taking his entire team off the pitch if any one of them were subjected to racist abuse again.

It was not the first time Houllier had made this threat. The previous season, just one week after England's trip to Bratislava, Liverpool had headed for Russia and a Champions League tie against Spartak Moscow, with their manager having left UEFA in no doubt that he and his team would walk if any of his players came in for racist abuse from the crowd. It might not have gone down well with the authorities, but to the Liverpool fans and, most importantly, the players it was a tremendous show of loyalty.

Interestingly, the FA chose this time of all times to announce that, while it would continue the fight against racism and hooliganism, it was also throwing its not inconsiderable weight behind a campaign to stamp out discrimination against homosexuality at football.

While an obviously admirable notion, quite where it came from and why it had suddenly become of such concern at that particular time is unclear. The cynic in me suspects that it was an attempt to deflect attention away from the renewed interest in the racism issue and the growing conflict with UEFA over the problem of Eastern European supporters, but who knows for sure? The only thing that is clear is that according to Soho Square, the game's traditionally macho image had been forcing players to conceal their sexuality to try and avoid persecution both from within the game and the terraces. This had apparently suddenly become a huge issue and one jumped upon by Kick it Out, which, as always, was keen to promote the catch-all idea of 'inclusion'. Despite this, two years later, there is not a single openly gay footballer playing football in the English top flight.

Of far more relevance, in the October Plymouth Argyle midfielder Jason Bent was racially abused in the players' tunnel at Port Vale by Andreas Lipa, an incident which received widespread publicity as a result of it happening on the very afternoon that Port Vale was staging an anti-racism day of action to promote its Valiants Against Racism campaign.

Just a couple of months later, Norwich City hit the headlines when its fans were accused of racially abusing Everton star Joseph Yaboo. However, although the abuse was mentioned in the FA observer's report, not for the first time investigations proved that the reality was slightly different, because the City fans were quick to point out that they had actually been chanting 'fat' rather than 'black' and their abuse had been aimed at Wayne Rooney rather than Yaboo. Indeed, the fans, ably supported by their club, were quite indignant at the accusation that they had a racist element and, ironically, received high praise when they helped police arrest a supporter who hurled racist abuse at Bradford City fans just weeks later.

Sadly, that praise did not extend very far beyond Carrow Road or for very long. For once, however, it wasn't the fans who came under attack, but the governing bodies. In February 2004 they were labelled as 'institutionally racist' in a report compiled by the Independent Football Commission. Central to this was the failure of the FA, the Premier League and the Football League to appoint more staff members from ethnic communities. They had a point. In fact they still do. As I write this, there is still not a single black or Asian member on the FA Council, something that Kick it Out is right to question at every opportunity.

With the upper echelons of the game now firmly in the spotlight as a result of the report, they received a further blow just weeks later when football pundit Ron Atkinson called Chelsea star Marcel Desailley 'a fucking lazy, thick nigger', live on air after the Blues' Champions League game against Monaco. Ironically, 'Big Ron', as he was known to millions, had been at the forefront of the so-called 'black invasion' in the seventies and was actually the manager responsible for the famous Three Degrees at West Bromwich Albion, but it was a career-finishing gaffe and Atkinson knew it. In spite of support from a number of black players he had managed, including Carlton Palmer, after apologising unreservedly to Desailly he quite rightly resigned from his positions with ITV and the *Guardian* newspaper.

Inevitably the papers went to town, placing the racism issue back in the public eye. Chief among these was the *Mirror*, which ran a long and detailed article about the failure of the game to address the lack of black or Asians in positions of power.

This shift in emphasis from isolated incidents involving fans to deep-rooted, institutionalised racism at the very heart of the game was extremely significant, because not only did it confirm what many fans had been saying for years – that the terraces were no longer the major issue in the racism and football debate – it finally made many of those same fans think about what was going on inside the closed shop that is the game's administration. Not many liked what they saw. The FA, however, claimed that it was leading the march in tackling racism in the game and said that ten per cent of its staff were of ethnic origin. It did not, however, add at what level of the organisation that ten per cent were working.

The beleaguered FA was, however, given a huge boost when, despite the usual pre-tournament hoolie frenzy, Euro 2004 passed without any major incidents of either violence or xenophobia involving England fans. Indeed, for once the travelling supporters were widely praised for their exemplary behaviour and their contribution to the increasingly positive impression of the English game. Sadly, the same could not be said of British holidaymakers who were involved in serious disorder hundreds of miles away in Albufeira. Inevitably, it was the latter that received the most coverage in the press, much to the disgust of the genuine travelling fans and those watching from home.

And it was here at home that the real progress was seen, with St George crosses adorning everything, from cars and vans to houses and pubs. While in the past such displays would have been regarded as almost xenophobic, now the flag was being displayed with equal pride by whites, blacks, Asians and numerous other ethnic groups, simply to show a bit of patriotic support for the England team. It is certainly worth pointing out that a survey carried out by the Asian newspaper *Eastern Eye* confirmed this with the news that seventy-five per cent of those questioned not only supported England but, more importantly, felt comfortable doing so.

Unfortunately, the success was not mirrored by other groups of supporters at the tournament, with a number of games witnessing serious racist behaviour of the type rarely seen in England since the eighties. The France versus Croatia tie was tainted by monkey chants directed at French midfielder Sylvain Wiltord by what was estimated to be as many as a thousand Croatian fans. At the same game, observers from the anti-racism group Football Against Racism in Europe (FARE) were outraged to see two Croatian flags bearing Celtic crosses – the symbol of the international white power movement – but despite repeated complaints the French police did not remove them.

Neo-Nazi activity also soured the match between Spain and Russia, when approximately fifty Spanish fans adorned with neo-Nazi tattoos and carrying flags bearing Fascist symbols were seen wandering freely around Faro, Denmark versus Italy, when Italian fans gave the Fascist salute during the national anthem and, worst of all, Germany versus Holland. Here, a group of German fans hoisted a Reichskriegsfahne – a World War Two Nazi flag which is banned in Germany – inside the stadium, while others gave the Hitler salute during the national anthem. During the game itself, Edgar Davids was subjected to a barrage of monkey chants, while the Dutch fans were bombarded with homophobic abuse.

UEFA was naturally furious. The tournament was supposed to have been something of a showpiece for its anti-racist drive, but instead it had merely highlighted the fact that in certain parts of Europe the problem was actually getting worse, something numerous English clubs had experienced on their travels.

In its defence, UEFA finally began to exert its zero-tolerance policy on racism and hammer clubs and nations whose fans caused problems. The Croatian Federation was heavily fined for the game against France, while Roma also felt the full force of UEFA's might for repeated trouble involving its fans during recent Champions League games. UEFA also made it clear that if the fans continued to cause racist problems, it would have no hesitation in closing grounds or even banning teams altogether.

Sadly, if this was meant to send a signal, it failed. Shortly afterwards, Red Star Belgrade fans racially abused PSV players and an Albanian man was stabbed to death in Athens in a racially motivated attack following Greece's defeat to Albania. At the end of September, Millwall travelled to Hungary for a UEFA Cup tie against Budapest-based side Ferencvaros and its players Paul Ifill and Mark McCammon were subjected to horrific abuse, which the club's head of security Ken Chapman described as some of the worst abuse he had heard in fifteen years.

Worse was to come. A week after Millwall's ill-fated trip to Hungary, news broke that Spanish coach Luis Arogones had referred to Thierry Henry as 'that black shit' during a coaching session for the national team. Thankfully, the session was being filmed and Arogones comments were not only picked up, but broadcast on a local news channel's afternoon news programme.

Although the Spanish FA later apologised, Arogones did not. Instead, he attempted to justify the use of what he called 'colloquial language' as being simply a part of his job and a tool with which to motivate his players. Not surprisingly, and quite rightly, Kick it Out led the protests. However, these proved to be futile for Spanish football was experiencing a surge in racist and anti-Semitic behaviour.

Domestically, the worst incident took place in November during the Copa Del Ray (Spanish Cup) tie between Cádiz CF and Betis Sevilla. A group of around eighty supporters belonging to the group Supporters Gol Sur flew flags and banners with Fascist symbols and chanted horrific abuse throughout the game. Despite a huge police presence, only two people were ejected from the ground and that was for damaging chairs. No one was detained for racist behaviour.

Just a week later the problem in Spain really hit the headlines when England visited the country for friendly fixtures at under twenty-one and senior international level. It had been suggested that the time had finally come to make a stand and that the best way to do that would be for the Arsenal players to boycott the game. In the event, the England squad decided that the best way to protest and show support for the anti-racism cause would be for them to warm up for the games wearing shirts bearing the Kick Racism logo. But it was a futile gesture as both games were marred by quite horrific levels of racist abuse targeted at England's black players. So bad was it, that England midfielder, Jermaine Jenas, claimed it was the worst abuse he had ever heard.

Condemnation came from all sides. Sports minister Richard Caborn called on FIFA and UEFA to carry out urgent investigations and even the prime minister voiced concern. At a footballing level, the FA lodged an immediate complaint, as did FARE, who linked the trouble with the comments made by the Spanish coach and the failure of the Spanish FA to deal with them properly. This sentiment was echoed by Piara Powar, the director of Kick It Out, who also registered concern that large sections of the crowd, including members of the Spanish FA and the press, seemingly did not understand what the problem was – an indication of just how far many European nations still had to go in the battle against racism.

The most dramatic response, however, came from PFA chairman Gordon Taylor, who claimed that since his members were being humiliated, the team should simply have walked off. It was, after all, a matter of human dignity. He then called on the various FA chairmen to make a stand and make it clear that they would take responsibility should the players take such action in the future. It was not a call that went down well at UEFA headquarters and the response was that leaving the pitch was not the answer for all kinds of technical reasons, not least because UEFA would almost certainly be faced with hundreds of cases of players walking off claiming that they had heard someone shouting something at them.

For its part, FIFA, through president Sepp Blatter, condemned the incidents and informed all and sundry that because the game was a friendly and was therefore under its control rather than UEFA's, it would be mounting a full investigation. Blatter then once again called on the global community to reject racism once and for all, yet amazingly, despite calls for Spain to be suspended from all European football and a UEFA-led commission to be put in place to deal with the continued problem of neo-Nazi groups linked with Spanish clubs (as evidenced by further problems at Real Madrid's Champions League tie against Bayer Leverkusen), when FIFA finally concluded its investigation, the punishment it handed out was a derisory fine of 100,000 Swiss francs (£45,000). Kick It Out was outraged and accused FIFA not only of failing to send a clear message to the game, but also of failing in its duty to society.

Inevitably, the indignant and almost holier-than-thou response from England to the problems in Spain attracted a degree of ridicule from certain elements and it wasn't long before the dark shadow of racism cast itself on the domestic game once again. Not for the first time, it hovered over the New Den. In October, Millwall had become the first club to be charged by the FA over its fans' alleged racist behaviour during a game against Liverpool – a charge which was ultimately dismissed – and so it was fairly obvious that sooner or later the club would come under scrutiny from the tabloids. It happened on 14 December when the *Sun* ran a two-page article full of allegations, which all but slaughtered the club and its fans. The only trouble was, it was obviously all bullshit.

In one of the worst and most inept pieces of journalism I have ever seen, the reporter, who just happened to be the sports editor of the black newspaper *New Nation*, not only implied that the home fans were racist because he had to sit on a row by himself – this for a home game against Brighton in December! – but in a classic show of ignorance he claimed that he had heard a section of fans clearly chanting 'Sieg Heil'. As any football fan worth their salt would know, they were in fact chanting 'Seagulls', the nickname of Brighton FC.

Leaving aside how this reflects on the quality of the sports coverage in *New Nation*, the fact that this was in the world's largest selling tabloid had a huge impact. Phone-in radio shows were besieged by irate Millwall fans desperate to set the record straight and the Press Complaints Commission received numerous calls and letters of complaint, not just from Millwall, but from fans all over the UK. To its credit, two days after the initial article, the *Sun* printed a range of letters from fans, some of whom had actually been mentioned in the article. All of them were angry – and quite rightly so.

Thankfully, the paper also printed an apology, with an admission from the journalist concerned that he had 'got it wrong' and was prepared to accept assurances that Nazi-style salutes have never been seen at the New Den and that there was no evidence of Sieg Heil chanting. However, it was weak, buried away on page sixty-seven and, although those who knew anything about the game understood that the original article had been poorly researched and ill-informed, the damage to Millwall had been done.

There was, though, a plus of sorts, as the fans' indignant reaction to the slur on their reputation did not go unnoticed. Equally, the club received a huge amount of publicity and long overdue praise for its anti-racism work. More importantly, as the game moved into 2005 it became clear that although racism had once more been placed in the public consciousness, there was a different sense of purpose, not only among those who were working to deal with it, but also among those who had to bear the brunt of it – the players. Many of them decided that enough was enough and that they had to be more overtly proactive in the battle against discrimination. In England, the player leading the fight was Thierry Henry.

Amazingly, even as Henry was preparing to launch his high-profile Stand Up, Speak Up initiative, the game came under attack once again, but this time the problem wasn't anything to do with the fans or even the players, it was to do with the FA – and all because of a DVD.

The idea was simple – to release a short, thirty-minute film called *Pride of the Nation* featuring the seventeen best England players of the last forty years, which would be given as part of the welcome pack to new members of the England fans' official members' club. Given the sheer volume of great players who have graced the English game over the years, coupled with the fact that black players had only really begun to make a significant impact in the late eighties, it was not too much of a surprise that no black players featured on the final list. Indeed, it is to the FA's credit that it was only once someone pointed it out that anyone at the FA even noticed.

Yet incredibly, people complained, not least England defender Rio Ferdinand who, while admitting that constructing a list of this nature was a very personal and subjective thing, publicly expressed that he was 'stunned' at the FA's failure to salute the contribution black players had made to the English game. Given that of all the black players who have turned out for the national side only possibly Sol Campbell would be anywhere near making the list, and considering that other omissions included possibly England's finest ever goalkeeper, World Cup-winning Gordon Banks, it seemed to be a fairly petulant outburst.

It was also something of an own goal for it angered a large number of supporters who regarded Ferdinand's outburst as nothing less than shameful, not simply because it was disrespectful to those who had made the list, but because the implication that the FA was racist was totally unwarranted. As an organisation it had been at the forefront of spreading the anti-racism message for years, not just in the UK, but anywhere football was played.

However, there were others, myself included, who regarded Ferdinand's outburst as being more cynical than shameful, because despite its record, the race card has always terrified the FA and by playing it to coincide with the launch of Speak Up, Speak Out, and secure in the knowledge that no one within the organisation had the balls to stand up for themselves, not only did Ferdinand place them on the back foot, he made the FA look stupid. The result was that the FA couldn't do enough to smooth over the waters and in what must rank as one of the most pathetic climbdowns in the history of political correctness, the FA not only caved and withdrew the DVD, it actually put together a new one featuring several 'outstanding' black players and even wrote letters of apology to everyone who had received a copy of the original and, most bizarrely of all, to the PFA!

The irony was, of course, that none of it was necessary, for by the time Henry went public with Stand Up, Speak Out the campaign was already so well organised that it was always going to receive all the support it was ever going to need.

Centred around the simple idea of empowering fans to show a personal opposition to racism and bigotry, the involvement of Nike was pivotal in the success of the launch. Not only did it produce 5 million black and white wristbands for fans to wear as symbols of their support, but a portion of the money raised was used to fund anti-racism initiatives across Europe. To support the actual launch and involvement of both Thierry Henry and Rio Ferdinand, the company also produced special T-shirts which were worn by players ahead of the Manchester United versus Arsenal game at the beginning of February.

More importantly, FIFA granted permission for the England side to wear shirts carrying anti-racism logos on the front and the arm during a friendly against Holland. This was the first time in 133 years that the national side had ever worn anything other than the Three Lions or a manufacturer's logo on their chests. To add weight to the occasion, the Dutch also wore a specially designed black and white kit for the game, rather than their traditional orange.

It all looked brilliantly positive but, behind the scenes, all was not well. The first signs of problems came at the game between Arsenal and Manchester United, when four players refused to wear special training shirts carrying the Stand Up, Speak Up message during the warm up. It is also rumoured that Arsenal midfielder Patrick Viera took a pop at Gary Neville in the player's tunnel as they waited to go out on to the pitch before the game, because the United defender wasn't wearing an anti-racist wristband.

In the days that followed, various anti-racism organisations began to question Nike's sudden interest in the issue and voiced concerns that the new campaign had been launched upon the game with little or no consultation with established groups. On top of that, lobby groups who had long campaigned against Nike for using Far Eastern suppliers who exploited child labour began to campaign heavily against the company. Their argument was that it was hardly right that wristbands made in third-world sweatshops by children being paid pennies should be sold to raise money to ease the hurt feelings of highly paid and pampered footballers.

There were also other concerns about money, not least where and how it would be spent. Many anti-racism groups in Europe have links to other political issues, including globalisation, and a number made it clear they would never take money from a multinational such as Nike, no matter what the circumstances.

Domestically, another row exploded among the England players ahead of the game against Holland, when England star Wayne Rooney began handing out black and white wristbands in the team dressing room. Not only was this done without FA approval, but a number of players were furious that Rooney had seemingly been exploited by Nike in this way. The following day an exasperated Gary Neville went public and made possibly the bravest statement ever made by a professional footballer. He said that he believed commercial companies, including Nike, were using anti-racism campaigns for free PR and as a result the issue was in danger of being cheapened.

The fact that an England international was prepared to speak out was astonishing enough, but when one considers that Nike has a £300 million, ten-year sponsorship and merchandising deal with Manchester United and that his United and England team-mate Rio Ferdinand had been central to the launch of Stand Up, Speak Up, it makes his assertion even more amazing, yet the simple truth of the matter is that he was right. Well, partially right, for racism and its impact on football has been exploited as an issue by all kinds of individuals and groups for years, but with the exception of one or two individuals, no one had dared to say anything until Neville spoke out.

Initially, the anti-racism groups and certain elements of the press were quick to jump on his case. Kick it Out accused him of complacency, while Nike refuted his claims, stating that 'the campaign isn't about publicity, it's about racism, and the fact remains that there is racism in football'.

Yet Neville also received a great deal of support, especially from some of the newspaper columnists. They realised that what Neville was really questioning was why there was any need for corporate branding at all. After all, as players, he and his many colleagues had always been happy to wear badges, support campaigns and even attend functions to support the anti-racism cause. They did this not out of any corporate duty, but out of loyalty to fellow players who had endured abuse during their playing careers. The question was, why should Nike be allowed to hijack that loyalty for gain and, just as importantly, why should the players help them do it?

Equally, numerous commentators finally gave voice to the opinion that the overzealous anti-racism bandwagon was so desperate to keep its own particular gravy train going that it alone had manufactured a false picture of the English game as still being a pit of racist-fuelled hate. Indeed, John Dillon the chief sports writer of the *Express*, even went so far as to say that 'now the bandwagon is exposed as something out of all proportion to the level of racism in the English game'. He was, as always, spot on.

Whatever the truth of the situation, there was, from that point on, a clear and long overdue shift in attitudes towards racism and the professional game – not from the fans, but from the anti-racism groups, who finally began to turn off the vitriol and instead began to highlight the brilliant work they were doing in the lower reaches of football. Sure, there were times when they flexed their muscles, but their anger was mainly directed overseas, more often than not as a result of racial abuse that was aimed at players from English teams taking part in Champions League or UEFA Cup ties. And for the most part, that is where the problems lie – in Europe, particularly in Eastern Europe.

There, the issue of racism on the terraces has barely been touched upon and although both UEFA and FIFA have finally started to get their act together, it is going to be a long time before they are anywhere near winning that particular fight.

Here in England, however, thanks to the efforts of countless individuals and organisations, it is one fight we can at least claim to have all but won. Yes, of course, there has been the odd incident over this last season and it is sadly inevitable that there will be others in the future. After all, football might have the ability to change the way we behave inside grounds, but it cannot always change the way people think. That particular battle is far from over and although football will always be a great and powerful weapon, it is a battle that it cannot even fight, let alone hope to win, on it's own. It can, however, carry on the fight elsewhere, for while our grounds might be freer of racism than they have ever been, the same cannot be said of other areas of the great game and that is where groups such as Kick it Out and the CRE really do have their work cut out.

Since they first came on the scene, there is little doubt that the various anti-racism groups have achieved amazing things with our national game. Within the world of professional football, for example, the issue of racism has gone from a horror story to a fairy tale in under two decades, with even the support of the national side finally being thought of in a more positive light. Furthermore, down in the lower leagues and in communities around the UK, the amount of work being done is simply astonishing, not just by groups such as Kick it Out and Show Racism the Red Card, but by the clubs and the fans, all of whom believe passionately in what they do and why they do it. And all credit to them.

However, while I am always among the first to applaud these successes, I have also in the past been extremely critical of some of the anti-racist groups working within football, not because of any political beliefs or because I disagree with their ideals, but because on too many occasions I have disagreed with the way they have gone about their business.

All too often I have watched the professional anti-racists create problems where there have been none, exploit situations for their own ends and damage the game I love for no other reason than to gain cheap publicity for themselves and their cause. Given the nature and sensitivity of that cause, this would have been bad enough, but to make matters worse, by continuing to criticise football they have routinely undermined the efforts of those people who drove their message forward – the foot soldiers in the front line of the war against those who for far too long were allowed to contaminate football with their vile abuse and actions, the fans. To me, that is unforgivable.

It wouldn't be so bad if I were talking solely about the past, but sadly I am not. As recently as 14 October 2005, at a meeting organised by Mark Perryman of the Philosophy Football organisation, Piara Power, the chairman of Kick it Out claimed that racism was partially responsible for the decision to select Peter Crouch ahead of Jermaine Defoe in recent England international games. On the same evening, a gentleman from the Turkish and Kurdish Football Federation talked about racism against Turks and somehow spoke for half an hour without making a single reference to the real cause of anti-Turkish feeling among football fans across Europe – the murders of two Leeds United fans in 2000 – instead preferring to blame it on his nation's history.

Thankfully, on this occasion neither gentleman got away with their claims unchallenged, but that is not always the case. This is almost entirely due to the fact that as a society we have adopted anti-racism as a positive and fundamental part of our culture and, as a result, have come to regard anything anti-racist as being unquestionably right and anything remotely racist as being unquestionably wrong.

This is a fundamental flaw. Racism and multiculturalism have become two of the key issues affecting the way we live, but by allowing the anti-racist and politically-driven lobby groups to occupy the moral high ground, we have become terrified of openly questioning anything relating to race for fear that we will be labelled as racist; a fear that is especially prevalent among the white Anglo-Saxon and Christian communities who, lest we forget, actually form the majority of the population.

As a consequence, these groups have been allowed to get away with things that they really shouldn't be allowed to get away with. We may laugh at the stupidity of banning piggy banks or replacing the seven dwarfs with the seven gnomes, but in their own way each act of petty political correctness drives the wedge between the various ethnic groups ever deeper.

More importantly, by suppressing a much-needed and long

overdue debate about the impact these issues have on us all, we as a nation are clearly storing up huge problems, if only because ignorance breeds fear and fear breeds resentment, which could, potentially, play right into the hands of extreme political groups. It doesn't take a genius to realise that the implications of that would stretch far wider than the turnstile or the playing field.

However, racism is an issue that not only should be talked about, it is one that we must talk about. Dialogue is, after all, the only way we as a society will ever understand things and we have to do that if we are ever to be rid of this most shameful of scourges. That will only happen when we are brave enough to allow everyone to have their say and, more importantly, listen to what is being said. Tragically, even though we live in a supposedly free society, I cannot ever see that happening. Indeed, there is something to be said for the idea that if Enoch Powell achieved one thing with his infamous 'Rivers of Blood' speech it was to suppress forever any chance of anyone having a free and open debate about either immigration or race in Britain.

Ironically, the area of society that has done more than any other to combat racism in Britain is football. In recent weeks I have witnessed racist abuse being hurled by blacks, whites and Asians in shops, pubs and even at a motorway service station, yet I can count on three fingers the number of racist incidents I have encountered inside a stadium in this country since I began writing in 1996, and two of those were at non-league games. And I'm not alone. Even Thierry Henry has been quoted as saying that he has not heard any racist abuse inside a stadium since he came to play in this country, yet still we routinely hear football being slaughtered. Why? Surely the fact that on the rare occasions an incident of football-related racial abuse takes place here in England it is roundly and swiftly condemned by all parties is proof of how serious this issue has been taken? Similarly, the fury with which we react to abuse targeted at English players abroad must indicate how far we have come, as well as how far others lag behind.

I'm not saying that we should rest on our laurels, but we shouldn't be so self-critical either. As fans, we should be proud that, for the most part, the only colour we care about is the colour of the shirt and we should celebrate the fact that people come from all over the world to play the game here free of the abuse and intimidation seen all too often in Spain, Italy, Germany and most of Eastern Europe. We should also be thrilled that so many black players represent us at international level, but, equally, we should enjoy a smug smile of satisfaction that these days we don't even really notice. All we actually see is eleven proud Englishmen and that in itself says everything to me.

Sadly, there are a select few it doesn't seem to say anything to at all. They want more, much more. Their list of demands includes more opportunities for black coaches, managers and administrators, as well as a British-born Asian player in the Premiership and a huge increase in the number of Asian fans attending games. Not much there then.

To be fair, in some instances they have a point. As I type this, the PFA calculates that twenty-two per cent of the professional players plying their trade in England are black, yet there are just three managers and a similar number of coaches from ethnic minority groups working within the professional game. That's shameful enough, but when you discover that the number of black ex-players looking for managerial roles within the UK is estimated to be seventy-five, of which eleven have the highest coaching qualification available – the UEFA A licence – it looks even worse. Things are equally bad, if not worse, on the administration front. Only Sheffield United has a black chief executive and, worst of all, there is not a single black or Asian face on the FA council.

Quite why that is has to be open to question, but there are certainly plenty who believe that racist stereotyping, in particular the belief that blacks are intellectually inferior, is a contributory factor. Not being a footballer and never having worked within a footballing environment, I am loathe to comment on what goes on in the minds of those who inhabit the boardrooms and the training pitches, but there is clearly something going wrong somewhere.

I would not, however, agree with the idea that this lack of opportunity is proof that the clubs have only ever really been playing lip service to the various anti-racism initiatives. Nor would I ever support the idea of positive discrimination, as seems to be frequently advocated by the CRE, the reason being that tokenism in any way, shape or form is fundamentally wrong and when we do finally see a black manager in the Premiership, the fans who will be expected to support him have to have faith that he got there on merit, rather than under some kind of government scheme. After all, there is no hiding place at that level and failure is beyond comprehension.

Exactly the same principle applies to another issue which sends the anti-racists into apoplexy: the lack of an Asian player in the top flight of our game. Indeed, I have to say I find the obsession with the issue of Asians and football both fascinating and patronising in equal measures. For while certain groups of people seem to be almost fanatical about it, I genuinely cannot understand why so much time, money and newsprint is wasted on this issue, when all the answers are there if you actually bother to look for them and apply a bit of common sense.

It is, indeed, a sad fact that out of 2.3 million South Asians living in the UK, only four have made it into football's top flight, while there are currently just ten British-born Asian players in twenty Premiership academies. However, from that point on, the whole topic becomes so clouded by tired old stereotypes and bullshit that no on seems to be able to see what is in front of their faces.

The anti-racists and even the Asian players themselves say that there are plenty who are good enough to make it, but the game not only refuses to afford them the opportunity to prove it, but for a variety of reasons it has actually marginalised them altogether.

Firstly, they claim, because there is a misguided belief that Asians aren't interested in football as a career; secondly, there exists a similarly misguided belief that those Asians who do play the game are either too indisciplined or too slight to be able to handle themselves within the professional ranks; and thirdly, because the majority of those who do chase the professional dream play in segregated Asian-only leagues and scouts don't bother to go and look at them. While there might be a shred of truth in what they say, it is just that – a shred. The rest is smokescreen.

As anyone who follows football will be only too aware, the financial side of the game is a disaster. At most clubs, the percentage of income being spent on wages is nothing less than a scandal, while for the smaller clubs, many of whom are yet to recover from the collapse of the ITV Digital deal, things have been made even worse by the drop in income traditionally generated by developing players and selling them on. This is the sad consequence of the seemingly bog-standard

Premiership club policy of hoovering up local schoolboy talent and tying them into long and exclusive contracts.

However, one of the few positives to come from this downturn in football's fortunes is that more and more managers are becoming adept at finding players in odd places and bringing them through on the cheap. Equally, absolutely everyone involved with the game at each and every level has become aware that it has become as much about survival off the pitch as it is on it, and that means a relentless and often desperate quest to generate income. As a result, sponsorship, corporate hospitality and club lotteries have become as much a part of the matchday experience as programmes and obnoxious stewards, while clubs work tirelessly to spread the word by working with local schools and community groups in the hope that it will entice people through the turnstiles. It doesn't take a genius to work out where I'm going here. It should be fairly obvious – and it is.

When Manchester United, the world's biggest club, signed South Korean Ji Sung Park, not only did the club gain a great player, but the commercial department at Old Trafford gained a significant and very lucrative foothold in the Far East, one it has been quick to exploit. Everton did likewise in China, when they signed midfielder Li Tie and the same can be said for numerous other clubs.

The point is, when two of the largest clubs in the land go to these lengths to tap into new markets, does anyone genuinely believe that they, along with every other club in the land, haven't considered the impact a twenty-goal-a-season, British-born Asian striker would have on their balance sheets? Are the anti-racists so arrogant that they continue to believe that clubs located in the middle of predominantly Asian communities, such as Bradford, Leicester and L*t*n, haven't even thought about the commercial possibilities a locally born player would provide?

Of course, the clubs are looking. They're absolutely desperate. The tragedy is that there aren't any there and if there were, they would have been snapped up by now. While those lads who turn out for clubs in the Asian leagues might disagree vehemently, the facts speak for themselves. The question – and it's a huge question – is why?

The difficulty here is that the search for suitable answers has been clouded by groups such as Kick it Out, who work tirelessly to convince anyone who will listen that it's because no one is looking. Only when you dismiss that can you come anywhere near finding the real reasons and even then it takes some thinking about, because there are all kinds of factors involved.

Chief among these is the simple truth that large sections of the Asian community hold values which place a far higher priority on family, education, religion and work than they do on sport. This is supported by various reports, including one from Leicester City, which confirms that the club has had some extremely talented Asian youths in its academy in recent years, but they have all been pulled out by their parents once puberty has struck and education has become more important.

In a similar vein, I've spoken to a number of people who have put forward the explanation that certain sections of the Muslim community frown upon participation in professional sport, because of its links with gambling and cheating, both of which are against the teachings of Islam.

It is also extremely important to remember that Asian nations have traditionally followed cricket, and to a lesser extent hockey, rather than football and, given that India and Pakistan have a combined population of 1.25 billion, yet between them couldn't field a single team capable of holding their own in the Championship, let alone the Premiership, even the most jaundiced anti-racist would have to concede that there might be something in that.

Since large-scale immigration into the UK is a relatively recent phenomenon, it is not unreasonable to assume that those Asians who came here arrived with little or no knowledge of the game and that must certainly have influenced the development of the sport within the community, not least because Asian fathers would have spent their time teaching their sons to play cricket rather than football, unlike the average English dad, who invariably makes sure his sons will be kicking balls around as soon as they can walk.

As a result, the first time many Asian boys ever really play the game seriously is when they start school and, when one considers that clubs are now scouting kids as young as eight or nine, that's an almost impossible time to catch up in terms of development, no matter how gifted the kid might be.

Now that we have more and more Asians playing the game that will inevitably change as they have sons of their own, but it will take time to filter through. Thankfully, signs are appearing that things are already changing, with more and more Asians playing to a decent standard at junior level and breaking into footballing academies.

This leads us into the controversial issue of attitude and the suggestion that if they don't get picked up by clubs at an early age, young British Asian footballers who do exhibit a degree of skill simply aren't prepared to put the graft in and battle their way through the traditional ranks to learn their craft and earn their way into the top flight.

Controversial it might be, but personally I think that there is a lot to be said for this. I watch a fair amount of non-league football, yet I can't remember seeing a single Asian player turning out in the semi-pro game. If, as the representatives of the Asian leagues continually tell us, they have players good enough to make it in the Premiership, it surely follows that there must be plenty who could do a more than decent job at this level of the game if they wanted to. So where are they?

The claim is that either racism or non-acceptance into the lower echelons of game keeps them out and, while I have some sympathy with that, it hasn't stopped hundreds, if not thousands, of players from other ethnic minority groups turning out for non-league teams the length and breadth of the UK. And let's not forget that the seventies and eighties players from within the black community battled their way through all kinds of prejudice, not just from fans, but also from within the game. Now few football supporters even consider them in terms of colour, so why are players from within the Asian community not prepared to do the same, given that racism is far, far less of a problem now than it was back then?

There can only really be one answer to that and it is the existence of these separatist leagues. While they would be fine for those wanting nothing more than a safe and comfortable environment in which to play competitive football, for anyone looking to gain experience and develop their skills in the hope of a professional career, this self-imposed marginalisation is a disaster, because it has inherent and obvious limitations.

Only when they are scrapped and the Asian teams take their places in the established league structure can that ever hope to change. And the sooner it happens, the better for all concerned, because then we may finally see serious numbers of Asians breaking through, not just to the professional game, but one day to our national side. It will take time for sure, but when it finally happens, as it inevitably will, it really will be worth celebrating, not least because of the positive impact it will have on the numbers of Asian fans walking through turnstiles, which at this moment in time remains criminally low.

It would be wrong, however, to assume that the lack of any Asian players is the sole reason for this. It isn't. There are actually many reasons for the worryingly low numbers of supporters from within the Asian community and in spite of the endless prevarication and hand-wringing the subject attracts, just like the player issue, it can be relatively easily explained. All you have to do is give it some thought, then apply some reason and a bit of basic common sense.

Central to the whole thing is the simple truth that clubs do not operate apartheid and there are no colour bars on turnstiles. British-born Asians have always had the same opportunity to watch football as everyone else. However, the sad fact is that just like large sections of the black community – and many other communities who live in the British Isles for that matter – the vast majority of them choose not to exercise that opportunity.

While the anti-racist brigade would love that to be solely because of bigotry on the terraces, they know only too well that in reality the only prejudice any Asian supporter is really likely to encounter is against the team they support – and that is no different for any other football fan, be they black, white or yellow.

In any case, it is more often than not the fear of bigotry that is the problem and that is largely manufactured and certainly outdated anyway. Think about it, if you'd been brainwashed into believing that grounds are unwelcoming environments full of racists and thugs, why one earth would you want to go, let alone take your kids there? Especially when the people doing the brainwashing are the very people charged with protecting you.

No, the major reason why the Asian community shuns football stadia surely stems from its relatively recent arrival in the UK and the fact that the vast majority came here with little or no knowledge of the game and, as a consequence, no understanding of how important a role it plays within British culture.

That is obviously changing, albeit far too slowly, but the fact cannot be disguised that there are people in this country who don't actually like football and, while it might be difficult for us lifelong obsessives to accept, you can't actually make them if they don't want to, no matter how Herculean the effort you put in.

That said, there are certainly plenty within the Asian community who love their football yet the numbers seen on the terraces remains criminally low. Again, the question is why? To be honest, this has actually been a fascinating issue to research, because many of the answers I've had have made me think long and hard about why and where I actually watch the game.

Like all followers of clubs outside the big six, my support isn't based upon the quality of the football, but is instead a product of loyalty, duty and habit. Furthermore, in most cases the team we follow is not even of our own choosing, but is more often than not hereditary. It's handed down by similarly obsessed or (vengeful) fathers in the same way as male-pattern baldness and, as everyone knows, once your team has entered your psyche, you cannot change it. It just isn't done.

However, how many times have we cursed our fathers or questioned our sanity as we've sat or stood among a few thousand similarly anguished souls watching our team get spanked (again) on a cold, wet Tuesday night, when just forty miles down the road, 30,000 people have been watching a team of Premiership giants play the game magnificently in a cauldron of noise and passion? With that in mind, if we were starting out on the rocky road of fandom for the first time and had no family loyalty or peer pressure to contend with, how many of us would really choose to follow the same path? Given the choice, who in the right mind would genuinely choose Tranmere over Liverpool or even Watford over Arsenal if they didn't have to? So why should we expect others to make the same mistake? Because it can't come as much of a shock to discover that they usually don't.

As proof, we need look no further than Euro 96, which saw a huge surge of interest in the game, not just among men, but also among women. However, having suddenly discovered the delights of the great game, few of this *Fever Pitch* generation of fans headed down to

Barnet or Oldham to get their fix. Instead, most headed no further than the nearest television, where, thanks to BSkyB, they were able to pledge remote allegiance to a club from the upper reaches of the Premiership who not only played better football and were far more glamorous than the club down the road, but occasionally won things. Furthermore, thanks to Andy Gray and his colleagues, they were quickly able to learn all they needed to know about everything from tactics to history without ever having to put in years on the terraces.

This glory-hunting form of fandom attracts a great deal of scorn from those of us who attend games regularly, simply because we know that being a football supporter is about much more than the actual game. However, even if we don't like it, most of us understand it. Some are even jealous of it.

Exactly the same principle applies to British-born Asian football fans. Many of them also came to the game late and, like the armchair supporters, had a free choice of team to follow, so most chose one based on the quality of the play rather than the location. Hence the majority, according to a recent survey, follow Arsenal, Manchester United or Liverpool, rather than their local club. Similarly, just like hundreds of thousands of others, they tend to follow their team on television rather than in the flesh. Not just because it's hard to get tickets or they have concerns about travel or racism, but because it's the way they enjoy watching their football. Who are any of us to condemn them for that?

There is, however, one fundamental difference between the two groups and that comes from the impact their choice of club has had on the game. For while that made by the armchairs has and will always be negligible, the same cannot be said of the British Asians, because that has been major. Nearly half the grounds in England are situated in areas which have a minority ethnic population of over five per cent and the evaporation of the traditional income generated from the local community has been nothing short of a disaster for many of the smaller clubs. That's why they are so desperate to win it back. Hence the frequent 'kids for a quid' and 'bring a friend for a fiver' schemes coupled with the tireless work among local schools and community groups. It's all designed to attract fresh faces into the stands in the hope that the bug will strike and they will return.

At many clubs, this work is already paying dividends and there is little doubt that over time more and more Asian fans will discover the delights of supporting their local side and watching the game live. However, you will never convince them all and, in any case, the game will only make real progress when it finds a way of overcoming a greater obstacle than the poor quality of fare on offer. Far too many families from ethnic minority backgrounds are on relatively low incomes and in terms of entertainment and value for money, professional football comes pretty low down the scale. Not only is it incredibly expensive, but the vast majority of it is not actually very good. Those of us driven by the obsession to attend each and every game know that only too well, just as we also know that all too frequent gut-wrenching anger that comes from paying a fortune for a ticket, only to endure yet another shite match. But that's the risk we take as fans, because we understand that there is always the hope that this game will be *the* game, the one we will talk about forever. And we have to do it. It's our curse. Why would anyone, Asian or otherwise, do the same when they didn't have to? Who are the real mugs here?

None of this is rocket science; it's just plain common sense. So why is it seemingly so difficult for the anti-racism lobby groups to accept free choice and economics as being the dominant factors when talking about the lack of Asian fans inside our grounds?

The answer, sadly but inevitably, has its roots in self-interest, egotism and political correctness. The anti-racists know full well that the problem has been all but resolved within the professional game, just as they know that the issues relating to Asian fans and players will solve themselves over time. But by continuing to deny the obvious, they can keep these non-issues on the front burner, which allows them to foster the suggestion that widespread racism still affects the professional game in England. As a result, this brutal untruth remains in the public psyche, which is exactly where Kick it Out need it to be, because that way they can continue to claim that they are fighting the good fight. And with the game so fearful of the racist tag, not only can they carry on these attacks unchallenged, but they will never be called upon to produce any results. As a result, the anti-racism gravy train stays firmly on track and they can continue to gnaw relentlessly on the hand that feeds them.

The sad irony is, of course, that the ultimately futile but seemingly never-ending efforts being made by the clubs, the CRE and Kick it Out to drag obviously unwilling Asians into local grounds are actually having a negative effect, because there is a definite sense of 'them' and 'us' developing among some supporters. They see the game bending over backwards to help and encourage participation in football, yet in response an indifferent Asian community are increasingly being perceived as ignoring what is, after all, our national sport. That cannot be good for the game or, for that matter, race relations, although it will obviously be great for the anti-racists who will see any division on the terraces, however small, as nothing less than confirmation that they were right all along. Maybe that's why they appear to be happy to leave this unrest bubbling unchecked.

It might also explain why Kick it Out have been so unwilling to become involved in another, far more important battle. For despite the fact that they continually imply that racism and football violence go hand in hand, they have never shown any inkling of joining the fight against hooliganism. Yet if they are really serious and if what they imply is true, how can they not be involved? How can anyone hope to solve one problem without confronting the other? The answer, of course, is that you can't, because it's a lie. Not all racists are hooligans, just as not all hooligans are racists.

So is this simply another problem they are happy to leave festering to further their own ends? Or are they afraid that if they do become involved, much of what they have claimed and continue to claim will be exposed as being untrue? Or is it something else? Is their refusal to become involved in an issue which affects every supporter, irrespective of ethnicity, an indication that they are not really interested in helping football at all, but are instead simply another group motivated by political correctness and only interested in creating problems where there are none? It would certainly explain why Islamophobia and homophobia have recently taken their place on Kick it Out's agenda, despite the fact that neither are major problems affecting football. If that is indeed the case, as I think it is, then it is absolutely shameful. And what makes it worse is that not only is it totally unnecessary, but it is also incredibly dangerous.

No one can be in any doubt that the success of the anti-racism groups at the top end of the English game and among the supporters of the national side has been nothing short of stunning. In fact, it could be argued, with some justification, that the game has led the way in race relations here in Britain and for that we should all be very proud.

But that success has only been achieved with the help and support of those fans who attend games regularly, the vast majority of whom are white, Anglo-Saxon Englishmen and women. By continuing to antagonise and alienate them, Kick it Out is running the very real risk of losing its support and that can only be detrimental to the future of the anti-racism movement, not just inside football grounds, but outside them.

With so much important work to do within the lower levels of the game, that is a risk Kick it Out cannot afford to take. More importantly, those responsible should not be allowed to remain in a position where they are able to take it. Football, and the millions of people who follow and play it, deserve better than that.

CONCLUSION

Over the years I have given hundreds, if not thousands, of interviews about football violence. Occasionally they have been gritty affairs which took a broad approach to the subject matter in an effort to explain some of the whos, whys and wherefores, but, more usually, they have been for bog-standard news items when I have been asked to provide some kind of response to specific incidents, such as the murders of Chris Loftus and Kevin Speight, or to comment on the latest development in the 'fight' against hooliganism. More often than not, the latter are no longer than two to three minutes in duration and so any contribution from me invariably involves nothing more than stating the obvious or reacting to some half-baked and usually ill-informed comment from someone who should really know better.

However, no matter what the subject or approach, most interviews have shared one feature, in that somewhere along the line those asking the questions will have been patronising. Sometimes, for any one of a dozen reasons ranging from the fact that I am the nearest thing to a hooligan the interviewer has ever met through to disgust at the idea that I have exploited my 'past', the interviewer will have patronised me. Being introduced as 'reformed' or 'former hooligan' while neglecting to mention any one of the ten books I've written is a favoured tactic. Asking me questions such as 'What would you do if your son became involved?' is another. All boring and pointless, but over the years I have learnt to deal with them and quickly move things on to what I want to say, rather than let anyone else dictate the direction of the conversation.

However, in the main, the targets are those seen on film, for within seconds of seeing footage or reading reports, and in spite of the fact that journalists are supposed to be reasonably impartial, most newsreaders will have immediately decided that if lads are fighting at football, particularly if under the flag of St George, they are obviously guilty of starting the trouble and are definitely mindless scum, bringing shame on their club, the game or, worse, their country. As a result, the vitriol directed at them is relentless.

It is stereotyping at its most dangerous, but hooliganism is clouded by more stereotypes than almost any other issue, and stereotyping has therefore become standard practice for the vast majority of the press and, as a result, the bulk of the general public.

To be fair, that is understandable. It must be extremely difficult for the average Joe to comprehend why anyone would willingly become involved in violence of any kind, let alone something like hooliganism, which is very much a mob activity. Factor in the illegality, not to mention the total irrationality, and the whole thing must seem even more bizarre to those who have no knowledge of football's culture. Clearly, only a brain-dead moron would want to be a part of something like that.

Once you think in those terms, patronising is simple, for it is easy to pigeonhole those who take part as being whatever you like, be it racist, thug or even dysfunctional, while remaining secure in the belief that you are better than they are because you would never become involved in anything as grubby as fighting over a sport. This thought process is aided by the numerous academics who 'study' hooliganism and who all too often reinforce the perception of the average hooligan as being the product of a working-class, impoverished or even criminal background.

However, such practices have a downside, because when someone like me comes along and calls that way of thinking into question by explaining that, far from being rabid thugs who get into trouble at football because they know no better, the vast majority of 'hooligans' are decent lads who, away from the Saturday scene, lead relatively normal and productive lives, or that those who fight on foreign fields are often guilty of nothing more than trying to defend themselves, they don't know how to process the information. So, invariably, they don't accept it at all and instead adopt a holier-than-thou 'well he would say that' attitude and accuse me and people like me of being nothing more than apologists.

The consequences of this reaction spread far beyond the newsroom or even the front room, because by failing to even acknowledge that things might not be as straightforward as they appear, any chance of a debate is immediately stifled. The result is that any hope of a solution to the problem vanishes. After all, how can you ever deal with anything, let alone an issue as complex as this one, if you refuse to even talk about it, let alone try and understand it from every perspective?

The irony is, of course, that in this instance there is only really one perspective that actually counts for anything anyway and that's the one of the hooligans themselves. Like it or not, they are the primary figures in this whole debate and, by definition, are also the only ones who can really provide a true and accurate explanation of why they do what they do. And while the police might claim that they are winning the battle against them, the stark reality is that they aren't. They are nowhere near. The boys in blue might well be keeping a lid on hooliganism for now, albeit through the use of some of the most outrageous and draconian legislation to be found on the statue books of any civilised country, and thanks to the hard work of a few highly motivated individuals the game has certainly made great strides with the travelling support for the national side. However, as fans we're still segregated, still filmed and photographed at every oppor-tunity, still herded like cattle whenever we have to travel to certain clubs and still treated like shit at others. Furthermore, many local derbies still require early kick-offs, pub closures and cancelled police leave, while the mere mention of England playing abroad is enough to have the headline writers reaching for their clichés. That's not winning, that's not even containing, it's keeping track. The culture of hatred that infects the domestic game and allows this most irrational of crimes to continue unfettered is simmering away as busily as ever and, sooner or later, it's going to explode again. It's only a matter of time.

Only when someone in authority finally understands that, and accepts that the reactive and suppressive approach to hooliganism has failed, will this ever begin to change, but over twenty years after the tragedy of Heysel we are still as far away from that happening as ever. How on earth can that possibly be?

Of all the questions I have asked in my books, this is the one that leaves me genuinely frustrated, primarily because I simply cannot understand why it's never even been asked, let alone answered.

Don't get me wrong. I know the real questions should be asked of those who cause the problem and that they and they alone bear the ultimate responsibility for everything that goes on surrounding this issue. But I also know that they only continue to act up because the environment that allows them to do so still exists and they will continue to do so until such time as that is no longer the case. That's the simple reality of hooliganism and therefore, like it or not, the onus must inevitably fall on the footballing authorities to ensure that happens, sooner rather than later. Unfortunately, the game has never seemed either willing or able to accept that responsibility, despite the fact that it really stands to benefit should it ever rid itself of the violent minority. Of course, the image of the game and the potential to attract fans who might previously have worried about the threat of violence would improve, but over the years the game has collectively been forced to pour hundreds of millions of pounds into policing and I'm sure most clubs could find far better uses for that money.

So, given that the public are being routinely told that the war against the hooligans is being won, you would have thought that once in a while the game would have been more vocal in questioning why the bills from the local constabularies only ever seem to increase. In the same vein, why has no one with any degree of power asked why the police continue to press for ever more oppressive anti-hooligan legislation, when at the beginning of each season they tell us that the arrest figures have fallen?

And it certainly isn't just the police who need calling to account. Why, after all these years, are the clubs still being allowed to continually put the general public at risk by admitting known or even suspected hooligans on to their property? I could go on and on here, but I'm sure you get the point.

The problem is that even if we knew who to ask these questions of, there is no one to actually do the asking. The authorities are so wrapped up in their own interests that they dare not rock any boats and the clubs simply don't seem to be bothered. This is possibly for fear of reopening the debate about who is responsible for the activities of supporters outside the confines of the grounds – a debate that might lead to all kinds of complications, not least financial!

In an ideal world, of course, the inquisitors would be us, the fans. After all, we're the ones who bear the brunt of all this, be it through higher ticket prices, segregation, CCTV, early kick-offs, pub closures and so on. But in spite of the fact that the sport is totally reliant on us for every single penny of its income, be it at the turnstiles, as targets for sponsors or through TV subscriptions, we don't have any say. The FSF might argue that point, but having followed the organisation's development and read its blueprint, it is difficult to see anything significant it has or, indeed, could ever achieve within the game.

Instead, what we have is a relationship which is all one way. Football takes our money, exploits our loyalty and abuses our support, while all the time treating us like shit and ignoring our interests. And because it knows that we are obsessed and that only a very few will have the strength to walk away, it carries on unhindered. If it wasn't so pathetic, it would be funny.

What makes the situation even more ridiculous is that there could never be any kind of solution to the problem of hatred within the game without the support of the majority of the people who follow it. Indeed, were the authorities to actually involve the fans in the search for that solution, we might finally stand some chance of actually making something happen.

That isn't idle speculation; that's fact. We've seen the power of the majority work wonders in the fight against racism over the last twenty years and the travelling support for the national side has undergone an astonishing and largely self-motivated transformation over the last decade, albeit largely thanks to the shamefully underfunded efforts of individuals such as Mark Perryman and Kevin Miles.

Yet much as it pains me to say it, it is fair to point the finger of blame for this situation directly at the fans themselves. As a wise man once said, apathy is the curse of the working classes and that has never been more evident than in the context of football. It's not often that I meet any supporter who cares about anything other than what happens at their own club and the vast majority of those are content to do nothing more than moan anyway. Those who are motivated enough to actually get involved and do something positive are rare beasts indeed and supporters willing to become involved in organisations such as the FSF are rarer still, hence its membership remains at around the hundred thousand mark. That's not bad, but it's a tiny proportion of the millions who attend games each week.

This apathy seems to be even more pronounced among those who follow clubs outside the Premiership. Indeed, it is worth pointing out that while the authorities and the media might kid themselves into thinking that we all care about what happens at Old Trafford or Stamford Bridge, the simple reality is that there is a very large percentage of football supporters who don't.

The irony is that they stand to gain far more from resolutions to fan-related problems because they, in the main, are more likely to be the type of people who actually get off their arses and go to watch their team play live, as opposed to being those who 'follow' their club via Sky Sports or *Match of the Day*. However, the sad truth is that most supporters at this level have more local and pressing concerns to contend with, often on a weekly or even day-to-day basis, and so the idea of taking on anyone else's problems, let alone campaigning for anything to further the lot of the prawn sandwich brigade, is almost laughable.

Of course, the end and sad result of all this is that the police are allowed to carry on treating football as a cross between a cash cow, a development tool and stress release, while those who reside in the ivory tower of Soho Square simply continue following the party line when it comes to anything supporter-related, because they know they will never be called to account. As a consequence, nothing ever really changes, which is pretty much what's been happening for the last few decades. In fact, aside from the move to all–seater stadia, which was forced upon them anyway, it's hard to think of anything positive the authorities have ever really done to further the lot of the downtrodden football supporter. Ticket prices are higher than ever, the atmosphere at most grounds is dead, thanks largely to designated seating, and television is allowed to shift kick-off times and even dates at the drop of a hat, which plays havoc with the lives of the travelling fan.

Equally importantly – and in terms of this book, more relevantly – on a domestic level the fact that the authorities have not been called to task with regard to the issue of hooliganism means that the problem remains entirely unresolved by the game and only partially suppressed by the police. That, in a nutshell, is why we still have this problem over four decades after it really began to become a major concern.

The authorities might well dispute that, but then again, they would. The evidence, however, most certainly indicates otherwise. For example, take my own club Watford, a club with little or no tradition of hooliganism. This season (2005–06) we have seen more police at games than ever before, while the defeat of L*t*n in January 2006 was accompanied by the largest police presence ever seen for a game at Kenilworth Road. Information received from other clubs seems to show that this trend is being replicated elsewhere and the number of banning orders being imposed appears to be increasing on a weekly basis. To my mind, details such as these provide as true and accurate a reflection of the current situation as you are likely to find anywhere.

So, given that, as well as everything else we have touched upon in this book, one has to ask where on earth we go from here with regard to the issue of crowd violence? In short, will the game ever really be rid of the spectre of hooliganism? If we were talking theoretically, the answer would be a resounding 'yes'. It doesn't take a genius to realise that the game would actually be rid of the culture of hatred and violence overnight if those who fuel the problem with their attitude and anti-social behaviour made the conscious and collective decision to stop. That, of course, is highly unlikely to ever happen in the current climate and so the only realistic and honest response to the question is 'no'. It is indeed a sad truth that football will be forever tainted with some kind of lingering hooligan menace, which begs the question, why?

The answer, and there is indeed an answer, has its roots in the fact that football is our national sport; a position it holds for one very obvious reason and one reason only – because it is so popular.

Each week, millions of Britons both male and female will play it, watch it, listen to it and/or read about it. Media empires are founded on it, weddings, christenings, funerals and even births are arranged around it and children named after those who play it. The men who have been lucky enough to forge professional careers within the upper echelons of the game have come to be feted as celebrities and are paid extraordinary sums of money, while the places in which it takes place are regarded as more important than the local church. Indeed, for many an Englishman and woman, football has become the only religion worth talking about.

So important is football within our nation's psyche that all other mainstream sports pale into insignificance by comparison. There can be little doubt that winning both the Rugby World Cup and the Ashes series were amazing successes and did wonders for both their respective sports and the mood of the country. But you know, I know and everyone knows that they will pale into mere sideshows should Beckham and co lift the World Cup in Germany. England will go ballistic and party like it's never partied before.

In fact, so big has our game become that the popularity of it now extends way beyond these shores. The Premiership, the clubs who play in it and even the players themselves are now global brands, each one recognised and revered from Beijing to Boston and from Disneyland to the Taj Mahal. Yet in spite of that, football remains fundamentally a simple game. We might marvel at the genius of Steven Gerrard or Ronaldo, but we also know that the rules they play to are exactly the same as those applied to the local pub side or a group of under twelves running their hearts out on the local Astroturf. That's the real beauty of football and it's why those who play it at the top level are afforded such importance. They are after all, fulfilling the dreams of everyone who ever kicked a ball.

However, if the players are the heart of football, the lifeblood are the fans. Without them, the professional game would not and could not exist, not simply because they fund it, but because of the other, equally significant contribution they make to it. Call it atmosphere, call it occasion, you can even call it obsession, but it's that almost tangible thing which gives soul to a football club and makes supporters return week in and week out, be it to Stamford Bridge or Edgeley Park. It's also what makes football so important to so many – and there lies the rub, because like most things which stir the emotions with any degree of strength, football fandom has a dark side. That dark side is called hooliganism and to a sizable minority of supporters it provides one of the game's main attractions.

That might be hard for the authorities, the media and even the post *Fever-Pitch*, Premiership-watching brigade to accept or even understand, but it is nevertheless a fact. For those involved with the terrace culture, being with the lads, wearing the gear and occasionally being a pain in the arse is as much a part of football as the pre-match fry up and the post-match pub. It's fun, it's exciting and it's also bloody addictive.

After all, why else would they do it? No-one forces individuals to become involved with the Saturday scene. They do so by choice, just as they remain involved by choice, because where else, other than perhaps the military, can you find the type of camaraderie, loyalty, drama and, yes, in some instances danger and even violence that you find within a group of football lads? The fact that it causes so many problems for so many others isn't simply irrelevant, it actually adds to the experience. Those police, that CCTV, those ticket restrictions... they're because of you, they're your fault. Have you any idea how that feels when you're walking along a street in a strange town with a group of mates? That's the buzz. That arrogance, self-confidence, bottle, call it what you like, but the bottom line is that it's what these lads live for. It's not because they're yobs or thick, but because that's the way they follow football.

People who don't understand that are in many respects missing an important point in that supporting a football club – as opposed to being a supporter of football – isn't simply about watching football. It's about belonging to something which will not only take you from the highest of highs to the lowest of lows emotionally, but which will almost certainly have an irrational and disproportionate impact on your life at some point or another.

It might be as minor as taking the mickey out of a colleague who follows your local, lesser rivals or as major as being overlooked for promotion because you don't support the same club as your boss. However it manifests itself, it will make an appearance somewhere, somehow. It's part of the price we pay. Hooliganism is simply the extremist extension of that. It takes the support for the team way beyond the norm and adds aggression and even hatred to turn it into something some would call tribal, but which really borders on fanaticism.

That's why lads are prepared to risk everything for their matchday fix' why those who leave or are imprisoned are replaced by fresh faces; and why old faces are returning in droves. It's also why the authorities will never be able to legislate against them and why the game will never be totally rid of them. Not in a million years. When the culture in which they exist remains so attractive and there is seemingly no will to drive it from the game, how can it ever even hope to be?

That is not, however, to say that things can't be better, because they most certainly can, but to achieve any type of tangible and long-term change would take a huge shift in attitude from everyone involved with this issue, and that includes the police, the game and, ultimately, the hooligans themselves. That process can only begin, though, when the authorities accept that only two things that have been done to try and combat hooliganism have ever actually had a significant impact, and they are segregation and CCTV. Nothing else, with the possible exception of banning orders, has worked. At all.

The authorities might well point to the fact that things are much better than the seventies, eighties and even early nineties, and indeed they are, but the reasons why have little or nothing to do with anything the game or the police have done in their ultimately futile attempts to drive the hooligans from the game. Instead, they have their roots in the tragedies of Heysel and Hillsborough, which made a lot of individuals think seriously about what they were involved in; the explosion of the rave and drug scene, which provided a new and even more addictive alternative for those who remained; and, most importantly of all, the fact that people simply got bored. Anyone who was around in the halcyon days of football specials, terrace battles and even Fila BJs will understand that. Wandering around backstreets trying to avoid the attentions of the police doesn't have quite the same appeal.

Besides, if the game's grand plan had worked, you would not be sitting here reading almost exactly the same words I wrote six years ago in *Barmy Army*, if not ten years ago in *Everywhere We Go*, and to argue otherwise is quite simply a nonsense.

So, what if the unthinkable were to happen and someone were to be handed the power to wipe the slate clean, take a fresh and uninhibited look at the problem of hooliganism and do whatever it took to find a solution? Where should they start? Like most things in life, if you look hard enough the answer is fairly obvious. If anything is ever to make an impact on this then the first thing we have to do is to forget the past – not just the legacy of the hate which has become so ingrained within our game, but the ill-informed stereotypes, the misguided anti-violence schemes, the irrational myths, everything. It doesn't matter why you have the problem, it just matters that you have it and want to deal with it, so it is imperative that you draw a line under history and move on. Fresh slate has to mean fresh slate.

Once you've done that, then the next step is equally obvious. You need to decide exactly what it is you want to achieve or, to be more specific, what you want to end up with, and that certainly isn't as straightforward as it might seem. If, for example, the sole aim is to stop hooliganism, then the answer is simple. All you really have to do is stop hooligans walking through turnstiles. It really is as basic as that. No one has a divine right to enter a football ground and, like any venue that is allowed to charge an entrance fee, clubs have the right to refuse entry. The lads themselves would very quickly get bored with travelling around knowing they wouldn't be able to watch the team they support and so there you'd have it. Job jobbed.

However, leaving aside the financial impact the sudden banning of significant numbers of individuals would have on some of the smaller clubs, such a tactic would have one very significant knock-on effect on just about all of them. English football is famous for many things, but one of the most admired is the atmosphere inside our stadia. In the majority of instances, the Kop at Anfield being the most obvious example, that atmosphere is a fantastically positive one and is almost entirely generated by the home supporters' passion for their club, their team or even their town or city.

However, not every club is so lucky and in some instances the matchday atmosphere isn't always so positive. Instead, it's generated by a sense of friction, which manifests itself in abusive chanting, aggression and sometimes even violence based on a dislike or even hatred of visiting players, managers and especially rival fans.

But in every case, whether it be amazing or dire, funny or aggressive, the atmosphere adds to the occasion. Some of the greatest games I've ever seen have been accompanied by atmospheres that were so hostile you could slice them with a Stanley knife. Indeed, it's fair to say that at some clubs the atmosphere is just about the only thing that keeps people coming back – that and hope. It's certainly one of the things about the game that BSkyB are most keen to exploit, because it's what makes football different from all other sports. The old maxim 'Rugby fans watch the game, football fans watch their team' is absolutely spot on and the vast majority of people are glad of that.

Yet no matter how it is created or what the feel of it, at the heart of that atmosphere you'll find many of those lads who flirt with violence, and that is especially true of travelling supporters. And therein lies the problem, for their wholesale removal would undoubtedly have a significant and detrimental effect on the quality of the matchday experience at clubs the length and breadth of the land.

If you doubt that, consider the impact made by designated seating. It has all but destroyed the atmosphere at some of the country's biggest clubs and all its done is make it difficult for the Saturday lads to congregate together in their chosen spaces. What would happen if they weren't there at all? Not just at places such as Birmingham or Tottenham, but at Cardiff and Stoke. Do we really want that? More importantly, would the game be the same without it?

The answer is a resounding 'no'. Without them and the passion they bring with them, crowds would eventually turn into audiences and football grounds would become nothing more than glorified amphitheatres, neither of which bears thinking about. Therefore, it has to follow that not only does the game have to retain their presence, but, in certain respects, it should actually be encouraging them. This is the exact opposite of current thinking, which provides yet another indication of just how little the game understands those who follow it.

So what exactly do we, as fans, want from our matchday experience? Do we, for example, want games to be accompanied by the kind of spectacle that has come to typify Italian and Spanish football? Or do we want something more 'British' perhaps? Something built on the humour, passion and pride that are already established as the bedrocks of our game, but something from which the anti-social elements of violence and intimidation have been removed or at least watered down and most definitely kept within the confines of the stadium. Personally, not only is that what I would want, but it is, I believe, the kind of goal that is at least partially achievable in the short term and could well lead to permanent change long term if the will were there to bring about that change.

Indeed, it might come as something of a surprise to many to discover that most lads these days are no different from the average fan when it comes to travelling with their clubs or even their country. They might well wear the clothes and walk the walk, they might even talk the talk, but in essence, all they really want is somewhere to have a few beers, a decent laugh and to watch some football with their mates. Furthermore, largely thanks to the internet, increasing numbers have mates at other clubs around the country and the opportunity to meet and catch up has become one of the great attractions of matchday travel in recent years.

So, while it might appear that the idea of a scrap is uppermost in the minds of a group of lads as they step off a train or out of a bus, the bottom line is that often it's way down the list of priorities and, in many instances, doesn't appear at all. So ingrained has the fear of violence become that many don't even consider any of that, nor do they believe that these lads are even football fans. This, however, is one of the great myths surrounding this issue, because the truth is that they love it passionately and unquestionably. Why else would they travel, year in, year out, following their often underachieving clubs?

That is why I am confident – or as confident as I can be – that given the opportunity, most lads would step back from the brink and embrace a form of supporting that allowed them to retain many elements of their own unique matchday experience, but from which those aspects which attract the attention of the boys in blue have been largely eradicated.

For proof that my confidence has a basis in reality, one need look no further than the national side, which, over the last two decades, has been transformed from an invading and rampaging army into something which is almost entirely peaceful, often hugely creative and almost universally welcomed wherever it goes. Imagine something like that at your club week in and week out.

However, mine is but one voice and the game would need to canvas as many fans as possible to ascertain the true wishes of the majority. That would require the establishment of something which is long overdue anyway – a properly administered fans' organisation. This in itself would be a huge step forward given the disdain with which the game and most clubs treat supporters, but in truth it is vital and wouldn't actually be too difficult to establish.

The FSF, though flawed, is already in place and if combined with representatives from the numerous independent supporters' groups and trusts around the country, would certainly provide a broad enough representation of the game's active followers, as opposed to Sky TV subscribers. One could even make the case that if such an organisation were properly and wholly funded by the game – as it should be anyway – individual membership would require nothing more than ownership of a bog-standard club season ticket. That simple move alone would ensure that every club in the land had a collective voice, as well as the continued and previously unavailable opportunity to contribute directly to the future of the game.

But whatever the eventual decision and however it is arrived at, what is absolutely vital is that the final say should be made by those in the front line, the fans. Anything other than that would be foolish in the extreme, simply because it would be artificial – and we've been down that route before. Designated singing areas, song sheets in programmes . . . they've all been tried and have all proven to be unmitigated disasters, mostly because we Brits only ever really go in for all that manufactured, Latin-style, banner-waving bollocks on Cup final day.

More importantly, the fans are the ones who would have to drive through any change and create whatever it is they wanted to create, so they would have to have absolute faith and belief in what they are doing. What the suits in Parliament, Soho Square and the boardroom would have to do is to provide them with the tools and support to facilitate that change.

So, assuming the fans have had their say and settled on what they want, and our fictional saviour has accepted it all, how would they go about making it happen? Well, at this stage the most important thing would be to ensure that each and every person involved with the game, from the minister for sport right through to the know-it-all who sits behind you every Saturday afternoon, were left in no doubt that what was going to happen was for the long-term good of football and that there was absolutely no room for negotiation or discussion. No matter who you were or what role you played within the game, you would have to be either with the majority or you would be out. Period.

Equally, it would be imperative to set a timescale and let everyone know how it was going to happen and, most importantly, when it was beginning. Not only would this let everyone know that you were serious, but it would also highlight the point that while reaching the goal of a violence-free game was going to be a slow burn, the decision to start the move towards it had been taken and the fire was going to be lit quickly and unilaterally.

That would require the involvement and unequivocal support of the media and especially the tabloids. Not only do they have huge influence, but they reach more people on a daily basis than the game could ever hope to do through any other medium. It is here, particularly, that our fictional saviour would really have to flex his muscles, for without the backing of the press the whole thing could potentially grind to an embarrassing halt very quickly, so each and every sports editor would have to be told that the 'with us or we're without you' mentality applied equally to them. Therefore, if they weren't prepared to provide one hundred per cent support for the campaign then their press accreditation would be immediately withdrawn.

There would, of course, have to be the odd exception, but these would be largely contractual. The bulk of the media covers football on the basis that it is doing the game and the public a favour by providing a service. Well, screw that. Can you imagine the *Sun*, the *News of the World*, BBC Five Live or even Sky Sports News lasting very long with a limited coverage of the great game? No, nor can I. More importantly, I bet they can't either.

Once this step had been taken, the next phase would be to target those groups who not only have the most to gain, but the most to offer in terms of facilitating the campaign – and the first on the hit list would have to be the anti-racism organisations.

That might initially seem an odd idea, but it actually makes perfect sense. As I have talked about elsewhere, football has done more to further the anti-racist cause than almost any other sphere of British society and the success of movements such as LKROOF and Stand Up, Speak Up means that they enjoy almost universal support and recognition from every area of the game and the media, both of which would be vital to a campaign such as this one.

Just as importantly, they have been down this road before. They galvanised not only football fans, but also the entire population behind their message and, as a result, enjoyed unprecedented success. That experience would be worth its weight in gold. On top of that, not only would their involvement attract support from organisations outside of football – the CRE being the most obvious example – but it would actually help to reinforce and even strengthen the anti-racist stance taken by the game.

The fly in the ointment is that, for whatever reason, the anti-racist groups continue to attack football for failing to attract more fans from ethnic minority groups and persistently (although mistakenly) link racism with hooliganism. However, if they have problems with the game, then one would hope that they would be most keen to play an active and perhaps leading role in something that would be taking direct action against those they believe are responsible, especially when success would mean a game that would be less threatening to those who might previously have stayed away.

If, however, that were not the case and they declined to take part, then they should be left in no doubt that from that point on their days of exploiting football were over. It would be a tragedy for sure, but the truth is that they need football more than football needs them and if they weren't prepared to put something back into the game that has served them and their cause so well, then good riddance.

Were that to happen, they might well scream blue murder and

would no doubt use the race card to try and attack football for marginalising them, but too bad. After all, we already have laws to combat racism in this country and most clubs have proven by their actions over the years that they are more than prepared to use them and, indeed, to police themselves in terms of bigotry. More to the point, there are plenty of other sports which have problems with racism, the majority of whom would certainly benefit from their presence. Let's see if Kick Racism Out of Rugby, Tennis or Formula One would have the same impact.

However that question resolves itself, the other bodies which would have to commit themselves from day one are the clubs. For too long they have been allowed to abdicate responsibility for what goes on and that would have to change, not simply because they would have more to gain than anyone, but because they are the catalyst for the problem. Hooliganism is, after all, carried out in their name.

In this instance, the question of refusal must not even be an issue. Involvement would have to be compulsory and if any club didn't like it, be they Premiership or Southern League Division One West, then fine. Goodbye and thanks. It would have to be like that. If the goal was for a sport free of the fear of violence and intimidation you couldn't have one club fighting the fight while another simply ignored it. That would render the whole thing futile.

Aside from presenting a unified front, the clubs would also have to provide their own fans with the tools to drive the anti-violence message forward, not only among their own support, but also within their local communities. Once again, we need look no further than the various anti-racism campaigns to see how effective that approach can be. But, more importantly, they would be the central players in possibly the most vital aspect of the whole campaign, because once the clubs were onside then you would be able to take the message to the very heart of the problem – the hooligans themselves.

At this point, we must reiterate the point that neither legislation nor marginalisation have worked, nor ever will work, against the Saturday lads and so the aim would not be to stop them, but to persuade them to stop. I am convinced that's the only sure-fire way we could ever really reach any kind of solution to this issue, so therefore the key is how we facilitate that. This is where things would have to get really clever.

Since by this point everyone would know what the game aspired to in terms of atmosphere and, just as importantly, when the change was coming, it would be imperative for every single club to let its supporters know that a line was being unilaterally drawn under everything that had gone on in the past. There would be no recriminations, no banning orders and no resentment based on history and, to reiterate the clean slate ideal, I would even advocate an amnesty on any banning orders that were in place.

Not only would this reinforce the fact that everyone was deadly serious about this new broom, but it would also allow the hooligan community to finally accept what most already know – that the scene is dead. And if there were any doubt, it certainly would be now, because the game had just read it the last rites.

Once that message had been presented to the masses, then it would have to be delivered individually to every single known or suspected troublemaker, not on a match-day or even within the confines of the ground, but at home or at their place of work. For the majority, that could be done in the form of a letter, but for the hardcore it would have to be done face to face, because nothing would dispel any lingering notions of anonymity than the head steward and local Old Bill turning up on your front doorstep. Indeed, such a tactic has been used by both the Dutch and German police in recent years with incredible success.

Tracing people would certainly be easy enough. Most professional clubs hold a database of their supporters and all have both security officers and FIOs, so identification could be swift and accurate. After all, who knows their own hooligans better than the clubs they follow? Most of them sit in the same seats week in and week out.

But however it were delivered, the message would have to be the same. It would also have to spell out a few other things, including, most importantly, the consequences of not heeding it. No one involved should be left in any doubt that, while all were welcome, the right to walk through that turnstile was under the simple and nonnegotiable proviso that it was at the discretion of the management. The by now hopefully ex-hooligans would have to know that while they would be welcome and had a part to play in the new scheme of things, they were under license and were being watched. Step over the line just once and they would be out for good. There would be no right of appeal and there would be no second chance and, just to make sure, the club would request an immediate football-wide banning order from the courts to keep them out, not just from their own club, but from everywhere. And, most importantly, they would get it. This would immediately put the onus back on the hooligans to behave from day one and, in most instances, I believe that they would. They would have to if they wanted to keep watching their football.

It is inevitable, of course, that there would be those who refused to accept what was going on, while there would be others who would try to push their luck. Similarly, there will always be games where passion spills over into aggression. However, once the majority of supporters were confident that the clubs were determined to back up their intent with firm and swift action, they would, I am sure, soon start to police themselves and the message would soon sink in.

On which note, the one group I have not mentioned thus far in relation to this potential renaissance are the police, and there is a very good reason for that.

As it stands, just about every single lad involved with the Saturday scene, as well as a good number of 'normal' travelling fans, regard the police as the enemy. Therefore, were they to be directly and overtly involved in this movement for change it would almost certainly trigger a degree of suspicion, which could only be counter-productive.

That is not to say that the law wouldn't have a role to play, because it most definitely would. For example, everyone involved with trying to force through the change would have to know that the police were totally committed to supporting their efforts, while those opposed would need to be in no doubt that the warnings issued to them were not merely empty threats. As a consequence, anyone stepping out of line would have to be dealt with accordingly, quickly and to the full extent of the law.

However, other than the bog-standard enforcement process, the fact remains that to avoid anything negative making its presence felt, the role of the police would have to be a secondary and most certainly a reactive one. In short, they would need to take a step away.

While in an organisational sense this would be relatively easy to achieve, the matchday experience would be a different thing entirely, because it would require a massive policy change on the part of certain police forces, not least because it would be a huge gamble on their part and placing faith in people has never really been their forte, although, to be fair, they often have good reason to feel like that. Yet however they did it or justified it, the bottom line is that from the outset we would have to see not simply a scaling down of the Robocop style of policing we currently 'enjoy', but the adoption of a less inflammatory, maybe even friendly, approach towards the game and the people who watch it.

Such a move would provide an early and extremely important visible indication that things were changing. And were progress to continue along the lines most people would hope, it would also make it much easier for the police to begin building a more positive relationship with the supporters and, ultimately, maybe even dismantling their matchday operations altogether.

That is not to say that we would or could ever return to the days of games being controlled by a handful of local beat coppers, nor that a time might ever come when the police wouldn't have to be prepared for trouble. Of course they would, especially in the early days, but in the long term the game should certainly aspire to the kind of low-key policing we see at other major sporting events. That at least is more than possible – or at least would be were someone to grasp the initiative and do something radical.

Really, that's it. It's not rocket science, just ideas based on simple common sense. No doubt some will dismiss it as a cross between wishful thinking and the ramblings of a madman, but if you think about it logically, something along those lines really could work. How many times do you have to look at the issues of racism and the reinvention of the support for the national side to understand that? Both were major problems for football in the past and while neither have been totally resolved, they are unrecognisable from what we had to endure twenty years ago. So what is stopping the same thing happening with hooliganism?

The answer to that question, like all answers relating to this issue, is easy, because there really is only one logical conclusion: the will to do it simply isn't there, not among those who inhabit Soho Square and, sadly, not even among the fans.

Instead, everyone involved with the billion-pound industry that is English football seems content to follow the same path, paying lip service to ill-intentioned anti-violence campaigns that have proven to do little or nothing to address one of the most serious problems facing the domestic game. That is both terribly sad and an incredible folly, because it is nothing less than an admission of defeat. And once you accept defeat, things can only get worse, which, just in case no one had noticed, is exactly what's happening.

For despite the combined efforts of the authorities and the self-serving television companies to assure the general public that things are going well, anyone who follows the scene will know only too well that there has been a marked increase in hooligan activity this last season. More worryingly, the spectre of trouble inside grounds has raised its head on more than one occasion with fights in stands, players being confronted by irate supporters and officials having to be routinely escorted from pitches. That in itself is a terrible indictment of the state of the modern-day game.

Quite what the future holds is, as always, unclear, but the World Cup is going to prove a major test in terms of hooliganism for football and, most importantly, the English game. If our supporters can replicate the trouble-free success they enjoyed in both Japan and Portugal, then UEFA will finally be forced to turn its attentions away from us and focus on Eastern Europe, where the real problems lie. However, should the influx of hooligans from Poland, Croatia and Serbia spark widespread violence in Germany, then it is inevitable that our own most notorious export will become involved in some way or another. It might not be by design or by choice, but it will happen and the consequences don't bear thinking about.

Either way, the stark reality is that if there is trouble in Germany it doesn't matter who is involved, because the impact it will have on the domestic game in England will be significant. It will almost certainly spark a further upsurge in interest in the culture of violence that continues to cloak our game and that can only lead to one thing. Trouble.

But it need not be like that. With a little bit of effort we could actually take ourselves to a point where the national side headed off to a major tournament without the country crossing its collective fingers and hoping to chance. Equally, that same effort could see us watching our clubs in an atmosphere not simply free of violence, hate and intimidation, but of policemen. Who wouldn't want that? It really could be ours. All it needs is the will to bring about that long overdue and much needed change. Where is our saviour?

This book would not have been possible without the help
of football supporters from all over the UK.

If you have any views on the content of this or any of my
other books, please do not hesitate to contact me via

www.brimson.net

All correspondence will be treated with the utmost confidentiality.

If you are a student requiring information on issues relating
to hooliganism, please contact anyone else but me.